GOOD SEX
ILLUSTRATED

SEMIOTEXT(E) FOREIGN AGENTS SERIES

The publication of this book was supported by the French Ministry of Foreign Affairs through the Cultural Services of the French Embassy, New York.

"Ouvrage publié avec le concours du Ministère français chargé de la Culture– Centre nationale du livre."

Published by Semiotext(e)
2007 Wilshire Blvd., Suite 427, Los Angeles, CA 90057
www.semiotexte.com

Special thanks to Robert Dewhurst, Andrew Berardini, and Jared Elms.

Cover art by Shannon Durbin
Design by Hedi El Kholti

ISBN-10: 1-58435-043-1
ISBN-13: 978-1-58435-043-9
Distributed by The MIT Press, Cambridge, Mass. and London, England
Printed in the United States of America

GOOD SEX ILLUSTRATED

Tony Duvert

Translated by Bruce Benderson

Contents

The Family on Trial

"If there were a Nuremberg for crimes during peacetime, nine mothers out of ten would be summoned to appear."
— *Tony Duvert, interviewed in* Libération, *on April 10, 1979*

LADIES AND GENTLEMEN, the book you are about to read will change your life forever. Never before have you encountered a text as rigorous, as relentless, as energetically malcontent or as disgruntled. So step right up, if you dare. The subject? The Sexual Order of the entire Western World. Using structures and concepts that parallel those of capitalist economics, Mr. Duvert will demonstrate before your very eyes what our sex lives really are: exploited, objectified, imprisoned, profit-driven... and, above all, castrated. And when you limp away from the experience—now aware of how crotchless you are—you will forever after look with jaundiced eye at everything you once held dear: marriage, the couple, the protection of children, even psychotherapy.

Wait! Don't put this book down. Tony Duvert's rant against these oppressions, which he somehow manages to sustain from start to finish at a manic, nearly delirious level of analysis, subsists on a much more exciting turbulence than the sex activism to which we Americans are today accustomed, with its shallow bromides about the objectification of women, child abuse or the rights of gays to marry. From a position that is nearly converse to these concerns, Duvert points a rageful finger at the strangulation of *pleasure* by capitalist shackles. He demonstrates that, in our sexual order, orgasm follows the patterns of any other kind of capital: it is commandeered by the State, which ensures that its consumption will always be tied to another's profit, and that any free, or pointless, expenditure of sexual energy will be forbidden.

A disaster from the start, given that sexual energy only brings pleasure when its expenditure *is* "pointless": as play, as experiment or as an expression of good feelings. Today's "good sex," however, is a voracious profit machine. Its tactics begin when the sex of young children is "castrated" in the name of familial order; continue into pubescence, when sexual energy is diverted, or "commandeered," with the help of contemporary sex education so that any sex outside the family will be thought of as "perversion" or molestation; and, finally, climax at adolescence, where the deformation of the sexual instinct gets its finishing touches by the artful mechanism of guilt, until sex finally becomes an investment toward future profit for the State.

And what is the investment into which our poor, abused capacity for orgasms will inevitably be put? *Baby-making*. That the cycle continue!

Who is Tony Duvert, and has he always been concerned with these issues? He has. But *Good Sex Illustrated* marks a dramatic turning point in his literary production. A novelist firmly rooted in the *nouveau roman*, he won the prestigious Prix Medici for his 1973 novel, *Paysage de fantaisie*, a year before the publication of this essay. The novels that followed after *Good Sex Illustrated* were no longer experimental in narrative style, going so far as to adopt a conventional realist (or "pseudo-realist," as he told an interviewer) narrative approach. It's as if the experience of writing nonfiction had showed him the importance of expressing his ideas as clearly as possible, and he looked back on his experimental past as a dialogue with himself. From then on, his writings would be turned outward, more overtly political and much more accessible.

Essentially, Duvert's analysis of the sexual order is in contradiction to most of today's sex and gender "liberations," all of which are careful to respect motherhood and the crucial social importance of nuclear family values. But it is the nuclear family itself that, after being exploited, exploits in turn, first through motherhood, and later through the authority of the father: it commandeers, castrates and twists the child's sex instinct into a sullen instrument of power in the name of protection and education. It isolates him from the outside world and portrays it as fraught with danger. This is, Duvert makes clear, the same system that has manufactured the idea of the stranger as the molester of children, just to keep the child from any outside influence or contact with a non-family adult who might have a chance of removing the veil of family enchantment. Such an invention (and Duvert insists that it is an *invention* by pointing out the statistical infrequency of violent molesters who are strangers and comparing the risk for harm from such people to the much greater one of riding in the family car) serves to deflect attention from the real psychological molester of children: the father.

Father as *castrator* and perpetuator of the exploitive capitalist system; *mother* as passive *baby-machine* that fashions *child marionettes*; *child* as *victim* of both, his sex crushed in the name of order, his chances for free expenditure of sexual energy prohibited: this is the grim picture that Duvert presents, using as data a liberal, cheerful French manual of sex intended for children and adolescents and published in the early 70s, a year before *Good Sex Illustrated* was written. Duvert analyzes this text with an obsession bordering on rapture and builds a narrative of nearly total sexual devastation. And because he uses this liberal sex manual for his case study, his text becomes a massive project in the construction of irony, at the very moment in Western culture when sexual liberation was supposedly blossoming.

This, in fact, is the great value of *Good Sex Illustrated*: its Cassandra-like shrieks of doom in the midst of a celebration of sexual victory at the dawn of our contemporary sexual mores, its spitting in the face of the good doctors, therapists and teachers at the moment they are tipping their hats to the "love generation" and congratulating themselves on their alacrity at guiding children through the twisted maze of sexual development. These good educators will be revealed by Duvert as so many spineless collaborators; so the question is, I suppose, whether, some thirty years later, Duvert's poisonous analysis can now be interpreted as an accurate, ominous prediction of life today, or whether his complaints have been proven to be somewhat off mark.

Both, in my opinion. Much more than, say, Orwell's *1984*, *Good Sex Illustrated* has turned out to be uncannily predictive. And just as Duvert implied, very few of us pawns in the game are aware of it. Take for example, his analysis of the bourgeois homosexual, who hopes by collaborating with family values to build a niche for himself in the exploitive sexual order, thereby positioning himself for a little pleasure. Such behavior has reached "epidemic" proportions today. Or the increase in the manufacturing of the evil stranger-sex-offender as repository of all our anxieties about sex, as a mask for our covert exploitation of others and to control, rather than protect, the sexuality of our children. Or our use of the family-values alibi in general to consolidate more and more privileges in the hands of a certain segment of the middle class.

On the other hand—and this is depressing—the part of Duvert's argument that seems off mark is that small aspect of it that is optimistic. He hoped that measures placing sexual choice in the hands of minors in countries such as Denmark, where the age of consent had just been lowered to 14, would eventually produce a generation—the next one—that would be free of those constraints that perpetuate the abuses of the sexual order.

Today's young adults are that very generation, and they certainly exhibit a greater nonchalance about sex than generations of the past; but are they any freer? They are, rather, a generation of disillusioned libidinists, who see little value in "unleashing" the energy of the orgasm and blame their permissive parents for dissipating the power of sex and endangering it with new diseases. Finally, there are certain phenomena that Duvert interpreted as symptoms of the oppression of the sexual order, such as a lack of concern about the physical abuse of very young children within the home by parents; but now that public attention has focused on these problems, it hasn't brought us any closer to liberation from the sexual order he described.

Even so, *Good Sex Illustrated* should be lauded as one of the more brilliant deconstructions of systems of capitalist exploitation. In that capacity, its relevance will live on for many decades to come. Once we have learned to look at sex as an economy, it becomes overwhelmingly clear to whose profit that economy functions. That is also the moment when many aspects of our own

lives that we thought of as the results of choices are suddenly rein-
terpreted as programmed stimulus-response patterns drilled into
us by punishment, lies and the withholding of rewards.

That said, I think that some brief remarks about the translation of
this work are warranted. In several key instances, a word that had
two essential meanings in French—one to do with economics and
the other to do with behavior—could not unfortunately be
employed with the same double connotation in English. For
example, the French word *détournement* can signify the misuse of
public money, but it can also refer to the corruption of a minor. I
was not happy with some previous English translations of the
word as "detournment" when referring to the *détournement* of
the Situationists, so I had to be content with the translation
"misappropriation," which is inadequate, but its full meaning
progressively becomes clear in the contexts in which Duvert uses
the word. Even a French word as seemingly straightforward as
aliéner, often used by Duvert to describe the effect of sex education on the young person's sexuality, also had economic
connotations in this text because *aliéner un bien* means "to dispose
of property." Additionally, *consommation* in French can mean
either "consumption" (an economic term) or "consummation"
(relating to sex and marriage), so I had to resort to the use of both
words in English, creating an association between the two as best
I could. There are a dozen other examples, and even the usually
difficult *jouissance* (does it mean "pleasure," "orgasm," "thrill,"
"enjoyment" or something more?) entailed extra problems because
of the fact that *avoir la jouissance* refers to the full use of a property
under the eyes of the law.

Building conduits between seemingly unrelated systems of thought is argument by metaphor. When such a technique is sustained to the extent that it is in *Good Sex Illustrated*, sparks fly, because an entirely new system of thought is being created by the synthesis. In most cases, this results in one side of the metaphor being reduced to ashes; and in this case, all of our assumptions about sexual innocence and corruption, marriage, birth, child-rearing and child education go up in smoke when they are applied to capitalist economics. This is why I have referred to *Good Sex Illustrated* as "nearly delirious." It is a ferocious, all-out attack on one of our most entrenched traditions. An entire ideology is being dismantled by the raging of Duvert's mind through every aspect of our sexual order. I hope you enjoy the ride.

— Bruce Benderson, Miami Beach, 2007

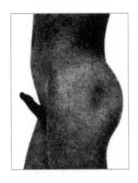

THE SEXUAL ORDER AND WHAT IT SERVES

A CHILD'S COCK GETTING HARD. This illustration is a same-size reproduction of a photograph that appears in the *Encyclopédie de la vie sexuelle.*[1]

This isn't an object of desire or an organ of pleasure: for us, it's a very rare document that will reveal to run-of-the-mill French-women, and to highly buttoned-up, run-of-the-mill Frenchmen, an obscure feature of a boy's anatomy. It's an extremely useful document if you can imagine being a man or woman and living for eighty years in our society, and even producing children and bringing them up, without ever risking much of a chance of seeing this. And I'm afraid that some men have forgotten having caught a glimpse of it on the lower part of their body, whereas they're closely familiar with their nostrils, their toes or their yellow earwax.

---

1. *Encyclopédie de la vie sexuelle; de la physiologie à la psychologie,* by (male) Doctors Cohen (gynecology) and Tordjman (psychosomatic medicine); and (female) Doctors Verdoux and Kahn-Nathan (gynecology); and by Madam Masse (sociology); with Madame Morand, psychotherapist, for the second volume, Hachette, 5 vol., 1973.

The photos reproduced here were taken from these works.

Like those photos that reveal the hidden face of the moon, this picture represents an elsewhere that is infinitely far away, almost always concealed. The paradox comes from the fact that we're not talking about some heavenly body in revolution 239,000 miles away from us, but about an organ that graces half of humanity, whether beardless or hairy; and about a condition of that organ that, contrary to eclipses of the sun, occurs several times every day and night.

It's a cute cock; it has a showy little glans, a foreskin like the nipple of a baby's bottle, a nice tummy for it to stand out from, a nice shape of thighs to support it; the balls are nestled between the legs; we don't get to see the rest of the child—legs, chest and head—because being able to would turn this medical, public-spirited document (which you're certainly not supposed to talk about like I just have) into something immoral, indiscreet and against the law: a face and an erection at the same time, being too human an image, are called pornography.

In the following chapters I have wanted to sketch out some analyses dedicated to the *sexual order* and the way in which it is passed on *to children and to adolescents*.[2] I selected the material for my study from this encyclopedia, because it's both exemplary and a new thing for France. At the moment when sex education is going to be doled out by the government, these works are presenting

2. In a next brief volume, using the same analytical focus, I'll try to tackle some risqué themes and other nasty subjects that are not within the framework of this book or only lightly touched upon within it: pornography, impotence, group sexuality, anal sex, prostitution, etc. I will use (within the strict limits of my resistance to the reading of them, which is trying enough) certain liberal-repressive texts on sex information intended for adults: journals, books, official publications.

themselves as so many civics instruction manuals, supposedly up-to-date and liberal (which is why they're being attacked by the right-wing press), but nonetheless intended to produce the kind of sexuality required by the Family and the State. They are written to match the age of their audience and those well-meaning educational principles held in regard today. That is what made the three first volumes (ages 7–9, 10–13, 14–16) so interesting as a basis for my work. The final volumes (ages 17–18 and adults) are more like the kind of sexology that has been sold for a long time in train stations and bookshops or in paperback.

These five works complement each other rigorously in terms of their psychological effect. The propaganda they undertake begins by exploiting repressions and forms of censure already acquired in the context of the family and during interactions in the child's environment. Then it adapts the subject to the series of alienations encountered while growing up, ending with the final stage: adult age, marriage, procreation, production-consumption, confinement within the family, obedience—state-sanctioned sexuality, which keeps all of it in place and will turn out to have created it: *good sex.*

I must make it clear that I haven't particularly wanted to lay into the authors of this collection, whom it would be unfair to single out from their colleagues. Each of them is merely an irresponsible and more or less clever transmitter of received ideas: the editors of the *Encyclopédie de la vie sexuelle* merely have the privilege of being to the left of what is published these days in this genre, and that is what points them out for attention.

In fact, the official writings of this type, whether "progressive" or not, get away from those who author them: they're actually a creation of the "silent majority," an offshoot of the conservative community—not to say an excrement of public order, a product of its foundations. And whoever attempts to examine these accounts of the social body will do well to put on the famous *écrase-merdres pour fiant de gendarme* found in *Ubu cocu*: they seem to be the reading instruments best adapted to works that were created by each side of the same ass: medical learning and the police mind.

Throughout this book I've often used the word "doctor" in a pejorative, or even insulting, sense; this was purely for utility in writing, and as a result it should be understood that I don't at all place the authors of the *Encyclopédie* and the doctors who don't share their opinions on the same level; I address my sincere apologies to the latter.

In opening, I've forgotten to make it clear that the illustration I've shown here was the only picture of a "member getting an erection" (as children are wont to say) that can be seen among the 900 or so illustrations in this encyclopedia by Hachette. On the other hand, there are about 60 photos of babies[3]—which ought to satisfy the immense public curiosity about them. There are a few unattractive and stony anthropometric nudes: the men have penises as limp and wrinkled as could be found, and our little headless hard-on is thus responsible for being the sole courageous representative of everything to do with "virility."

Not that "the opposite sex" is better treated by medical Puritanism. Indeed, there is no photograph of a vulva, except for the very chaste pubes of a little girl and, well sealed off under a haze of fur, a few female groins; but there are 26 brutally realistic photos

---

3. I am counting only images where the baby is alone: those in which he appears in a situation (thighs of mother, arms of parents, the family circle, etc.) are also very numerous.

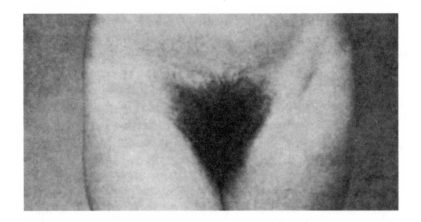

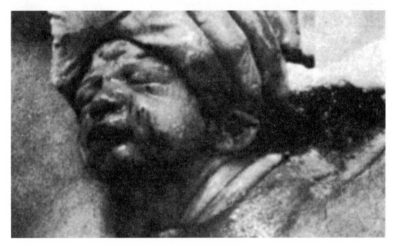

of childbirth, in which cunts finally appear—distended by the slimy newborn they're expulsing.

I'd like to point out, quickly and without any complications, the way in which order in a society of exploitation is based on the misappropriation of bodies—a phenomenon illustrated most directly by the sexual order. I hope that no one holds it against me if I now summarize certain ideas that different authors have maintained or could have maintained under a much more coherent form, using more valid terms.

It seems as if human communities are formed merely to assure the well-being of certain individuals to the detriment of all others. Life in society offers ordinary mortals the meager advantage of being destroyed by man rather than by the harshness of the environment. The sciences devoted to the study of human societies, whether primitive or civilized, current or past, therefore tell us, each in their own language, who exploits whom, under what pretext, using what means, which ideology or belief, to what ends, for what consequences, what profit, and how this maximum order is kept in place altered or unchanged generation after generation, in order to resist every attack, and how it is perfected to an excessive and ruinous point.

Thus, the narrow frameworks of our sex life are constructed according to rules and prohibitions that vary from one society or one period to another but always aim for same goal: *capitalizing bodies* and exploiting them. A society that exploits people needs by definition a rigorous sexual order, without which no misappropriation, no commandeering, no slavery, no privilege, no decisive and lasting injustice would be possible.

We devote ourselves to a large variety of actions, in which what's useful and productive competes with what's unproductive and superfluous: and there are at least as many "squanderings" as investments in our corporeal economy. Compared to useful expenditure, which produces or harnesses something, "free" expenditure (outside of any theory about it) is very original: as celebration, play, pleasure, it generates no "good," yields no profit; it isn't recovered or handed down, it doesn't even work toward our biological health; and its only justification, if it needs one, is the pleasure it brings.

Among these expenditures, the easiest, the most abundant, the most banal and the most recuperable is "sexual" activity. There's an enormous disproportion between our capacity for sexual expenditure and the intermittent, very modest needs of reproduction: our body is, in this capacity, an underdetermined erotic machine, which produces "needless" desire, pleasure with no sequel, energy without function that is perpetually expendable and reconstituted. Humans are permanently provided with a "surplus of sexuality" that they can discharge anywhere at all and whose immediate expenditure, contrary to other muscular or nervous activities, is a pleasure sufficient in itself.

This ability, and the need that comes along with it, take a particular turn in nonegalitarian societies: monopolizing pleasure, giving themselves the means to enjoy it more while exploiting others is, and obviously remains, the affair of certain men—or should we say all, though few succeed. Through them prosper the structures of exploitation that so many societies have in common.

Man is only exploitable if he produces something; the golden rule of a society of exploitation will therefore be: all expenditure must produce. Sexual expenditure becomes what is most severely restrained, since it's unproductive. It's organized so that it remains chained to profit: reproduction of the exploited, a market of pleasures and sexual objects, and especially the handing down of goods or powers that were made to support family structures established to that end.

In these cases, the powerful members of the group secure the most extensive privileges; they stabilize them: ownership of people, the means of production and products; right to control and virtually limitless repression; codes that formalize their power; institutions that petrify it and, in some way, distribute it; myths that legitimize it, exploiting the unknown and the fear of the Outside, encouraging the least strong not to desert the group, blinding them to their servitude and inventing justifications for what they're suffering. The rituals of sexual ownership that have been reported in certain packs of monkeys, in which the older males exert against the younger an exaggerated right to females, ironically illustrate the nature of the capitalization of bodies and the rule of maximum pleasure. It's true, at least, that the older monkey doesn't make those whom he is inhibiting do any work; he prevents a sexual expenditure, but he doesn't recuperate it. Should he ever achieve this ("exploitative" behavior has already been observed among monkeys), the planet will have a new society that is altogether worthy of ours. Because it's precisely this inordinate animalism that industrial society has baptized "civilization."

A human being that you want to exploit is like a source that you harness; his body is commandeered and enslaved, his expenditures are channeled, he's deprived of sexual satisfaction and plugged to machines and behaviors that will use, for the profit of a third, the expended energy. There will exist a system of permissions and prohibitions, values and beliefs that will define how the exploited must, on every occasion, plug in his body and invest his energy. The individual story of each of us, starting at birth, is one of misappropriations that have been inflicted upon us; because a humble human being is a voracious engine of pleasure, an extraordinary squanderer of himself; and to educate him according to our norms—to socialize him to a high degree—is to teach him to withhold himself and to save, as well as to point out to him the "good" investments. These artificial activities of desire and production recuperate the subject in full; in compensation, a minimal part will be given back to him that will help him to survive and to believe that the investments into which he has been forced are actually good.

A sorcerer who claims that paid-for magic practices can heal a sick person, recover livestock, bring luck to a harvest or hunt, make a woman fertile, etc., takes advantage of the same system of misappropriation. The expenditure undertaken by his client is carried out in pure loss; but the beliefs that he has received from the group tell him that such an expenditure is fruitful and that, if the investment fails, it's because the expenditure wasn't enough, or that the service requested is beyond the power of all possible expenditure, or that he himself, the client, is an obstacle to the process that should have satisfied him. In such a case, institutionalized deception consists of two stages: learning that "all expenditure must produce"; and incentive for an expenditure that produces nothing, but from which a third profits, and which enforces a social order. Conforming to this is a fundamental condition for belonging to the group, a proof of that belonging, a way of confirming the covenant and perpetuating the order.

Providers of imaginary services in contemporary society take action using the same mechanism: suppliers of prayers and deities, psychotherapies, beauty care, fashion, funeral services, every kind of advice, insurance, education; mass media, learning, vacations, etc. Most of these people are, for good reason, on the side of the exploiting order, although they hold only average privileges and lateral functions, like vultures keeping an eye on a flock, and it's common to compare them to these carrion-feeders.

An example of a more interesting misappropriation, because it's a matter of a very pure capitalization of the *body*, is the galley. The galley slave remains, in our metaphors, the model for the slave. Who was it? A man reduced to a muscle machine and plugged to oars. The energy produced under duress operated the oars and moved the boat. This boat carried owners, property, the powerful or their power. The goal of travel was profit. The galley-slave-motor was therefore condemned to a forced investment, a production of energy at the interior of a machine of misappropriation that functioned for the merchant or for the State. The grounds for condemnation were theft or minor offence—attacks on the order of the exploiting society. These acts were assessed according to their perpetrator and his relationship to established privileges. The thief, for example, commits an injustice outside the forms of injustice anticipated by law, within which theft is an inalienable right for the wealthy and their acolytes; a right that is only maintained if that class guards that exclusive right to injustice, while guaranteeing to the exploited that they will only suffer their part of it under certain forms and for their own good—a strange deal, may we add in passing. Thus, the delinquent from the exploited classes had accomplished a nonregulation act, which was both illegal and illegitimate: he was severely punished. The delinquent from the exploitive classes, on the other hand, had merely come from the context of a legal injustice to which he had a right: his punishment was light, if there was one. As you can see, things haven't changed.

If, in a society, abuse is the only hope for prosperity and enjoyment, all men will devote themselves to it, each according to the powers he has at hand. And theft, fraud, exploitation of another by any means and through every disguise will be an inevitable temptation for the exploited themselves, using the maneuvers that have victimized both. In addition, the constant *loss* experienced by the exploited person leads him to take abusive advantage of his social function and the microexploitations over which the State allows him some power: exploitations of the servant, women, children, the family, animals, foreigners, etc. If these small powers represent a real way for him to make up for his losses, the exploited person will accept and support these institutional solutions and invest in them what he has left of his desire. He'll become an owner of men and objects. And for this the family is a system that serves a double function: it offers the exploited a human reservoir for "recharging"—something to vampirize, as it were; and at the same time it serves as a reproductive cell of the outside order.

Apparently, a very long time ago, the exploitive order followed the dictates of a dangerous empiricism, which crudely revealed the abuses it perpetrated and the thrills of its beneficiaries. We would devour with our fangs bared, squander great floods of what we'd misappropriated, seek out new territories where blood would flow even more freely; we competed arbitrarily, with cruelty and at whim. Nowadays, this order tends to become "scientific": it seals itself off, it buries its booty, it pinches its mouth and tightens its anus, it wears itself out and wastes away in order to rule ever more relentlessly, it's excessive and small at the same time; it becomes aware of what it's doing and learns—especially through the human and social sciences—how to do it better. Such scientific capitalism is aiming for a stability that would finally shelter it from revolts, reforms, changes and lock it into that permanent social crisis that amounts to man's exploitation of man. It can achieve this by strict control of the actions and existences of everyone who is exploited, as is already done, for example, by Communist societies, and for the same reasons. But such control is difficult, and those who are exploited must maintain it themselves, by policing and spying on each other. To the extent that, for a subject, the pressures are personified into a detestable external power, a conflict is possible and the structure of abuse is in danger. On the other hand, if the pressures are accepted by the subject, if he channels his impulses into them, if he appeases his needs in them, if he uses them to satisfy his own temptations for abusing others, if he closes the circle by bringing to bear all these repressions on himself while verifying that others are also doing it, a perfect, invisible and self-reproducing system of repression becomes available. The police and their medical equivalents must now control only the margins of the social system, where, as tradition has it, the failures in conditioning take refuge—the non-exploitable, those who have kept too much or too little of their brain and body, and are dangerous not because they represent a real power against the Power, but because they perpetuate, more or less despite themselves, the undesirable presence of freedom.

The modes of action of the extraordinary excess of order that characterizes contemporary society are above all indirect. Power only turns to physical force and armed violence as a last resort; it prefers recourse to a network of generalized conditioning that teaches useful social behavior, allowed desires, accepted pleasures, investments that are "fruitful"—*the Order of Expenditure*, thanks to which everything returns to the same machine of exploitation. The fellow who has a profession, a family, children, friendships, leisure, real estate, industrial consumer possessions, religious or political convictions, succeeds in misappropriating himself relentlessly, which makes him the victim, the accomplice and the beneficiary of the exploitive order all at the same time. The scientific society wants totalitarian direction of the acts and modes of expenditure of the exploited, while increasingly hiding from them why and how it does it. Using the countless faces of constant propaganda, the State imposes, directly or indirectly, the norms, codes and values that regulate this slavery. Since the adherence of each depends on his belief in the profitability of the personal investments recommended for him, it's essentially under the form of objects of desire that the ideology is spread and assimilated; private property is that parody of pleasure, drawn from a product that is itself parodic, fabricated and sold for the profit of the misappropriationist. Having fallen deeply into the trap, the exploited-consumer compensates symbolically for what he lacks by collaborating with the order that keeps him in bondage, he lives and dies in the constant unreality of what he is doing, of what he desires, of what he has. Because the sole "reality" is external, it is in the hands of those who hold a power, it is this power itself. And it no longer matters that some "fanatics" preach revolution, or defection: because the majority who uphold the order definitely do not do it out of simple wickedness, out of interest or out of stupidity, but because they are irremediably adapted to it, like sardines are to their can; and when they find themselves with their heads cut off, grilled and drenched in oil, it's a bit late to announce to them that their life is going to change.

Ideology defines which individuals we are supposed to be, to which objects our consciousness is entitled, which relationships to others we must have, which ideal we are to pursue, which feelings we are to cultivate, which values we are to respect, which reality we are to share, and which images of forbidden objects we must repress; it tells us who Mankind is, what Nature is, and why Industrial Society is our Salvation. It misappropriates our entire body, all our energy, harnesses and disposes of the remnants of our desire and freedom, and confines them in codes that will bend us to the limits, toward objects and forms of action useful to those who dominate us.

The ultimate goal of conditioning is to blind our mind as much as possible to these manipulations and keep us from foreseeing any of them. For most people, this result is achieved; sometimes they retain the vague impression of being "exploited" (it's simply a word for a mood) when they're working, but they honestly feel "free" (it's purely a state of mind) when they aren't working. However, each minute of their life, each gesture, each thought, each desire, each belief, or even each revolt is produced by the system and represents the fundamental condition of permanent exploitation that they are enduring, at work or not. This is why a subversion that doesn't, above all, attack learned subjectivity (forms of self-awareness, perception, one's relation to the other, desire, sexual expenditure...) only succeeds at making the old order reappear under a new aspect. Because the reproductive machines that the order has invented and distributed everywhere are not the rulers, the armies, the police, the powerful, the institutions, the laws: they are our own brains. Cut off the head of the order and save ours; the order grows back again.

But a lot of dissidents would be surprised to learn that their little mind drunk on anarchy is trapped. As for the honest Communist worker, who, returning from his militancy, rejoins his patriarchal, highly submissive family: he would be indignant if he was told that this Order-at-Home is working for the employers and guaranteeing their future. The menial chore of producing slaves is always slaves' work: they are totally reliable *moulds*—even if from time to time, because of over-zealousness, they fabricate a boss.

In a more laughable order of ideas, we have people who, knowing that our food is toxic, buy natural foods at high prices; then they go gorge themselves on television, films, the radio, novels, newspapers or pop music. This is watching out for small poisons so that you can better swallow the big ones; or, out of fear of the policeman in his cocked hat, only receiving plainclothes cops in your home.

Beyond work, social activities and private ownership that is more or less phantasmal, and on which he'll have shed the main part of the energy that has been snatched from him, the exploited person will sometimes keep a small sexual surplus, a libidinal detritus that he'll deem to be very precious but that obviously isn't free either: it is to be spent on amorous behaviors that are profitable for the State and stipulated by it.

Permissible "orgasm" is an ultimate form of *goods* that you obtain through an infinity of obstacles and that you jealously guard. Because if pleasure remained without purpose, it would be the kind of squandering that thwarts the social order and the inner order of the subject. The *free* play of pleasure isn't marketable, it isn't invested to acquire, it wants neither ownership nor any permanent object, and it has no jurisdiction: it is gratuitous, and therefore irretrievable by the exploitive order.

Under such conditions, it remains prohibited. And the idea of the "sexual" that liberal propaganda, and the medicine that serves it, present to us as "spontaneous," as "natural," as the "animal" in us, is in reality that which is heavily influenced by the most rigid structures of abuse and the most subtle misappropriations. Our desire, our capacity for expenditure are what the system recuperates and exploits: our "sex" is that *conditioned vestige* it returns to us. These are the maneuvers hidden behind the ideology of the "natural."

A well-socialized sexual relationship will be the *market* par excellence, whereby goalless expenditure is transformed into an exchange that has interest, into a *reciprocal return*, and into a *relation of power* between partners who have anxiously evaluated one another to be sure that the swap will be profitable.

The squandering of desire is stifled by a familial/conjugal machine of endless production-consumption—the child of which is by definition what is at stake and the victim. This is what I will now attempt to illustrate.

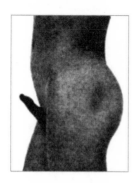

THE PRINCIPLE OF SEX EDUCATION

IN A LOT OF GENERAL BOOKSTORES, books on sex education are now presented with works for young people, graphic novels and cartoons, illustrated books, school publications, boy-scout novels, etc. If the volumes are well displayed, many of the young people walking by stop and look at them—but as a novelty that is suspect. In fact, until now, all that was intended for them were those pink biology manuals that the enlightened middle class offered their children, who discovered in this way how babies are born. As for teenagers, they could attempt to buy books for adults; but in principal, they were forbidden sex information. Suddenly, here they are for sale: and what arouses the suspicions of the customers I've seen is probably the division of this merchandise into age-appropriate slices. Such discrimination signifies too clearly that the books are keeping to what's allowed to be said. For physiology, they brazenly offer a massive amount of difficult information; however, when it comes to the "sex life," they are simplistic, and, torn between what's left of scientific honesty and the obligation to respect the morality of families, keep to the edge of what the minor himself already knows.

It's clear that the medicalization of sex information is nothing more than science taking charge of the old moral order, reworked according to some liberal principles of public health, with the essential prohibitions unchanged.

This could have been predicted, since life in society hasn't changed, either. And the imposture is that the books claim to make up for a shortage of *information* for an audience whose real lack is sexual *activity*. Therefore, teenagers glance through the books intended for those older than them, and they disregard the gynecological diagrams, all the various kinds of fetuses, the couplings shown in color cross-sections—in favor of a few photos of naked women and some idealized (I mean delicately unfocused) cunts. At least those images have a certain relationship to their frustration— which the educational discourse, for its part, understandingly acknowledges, but just to show which inviolable principle of psychic health justifies it. Prevented from having sex, minors will now know that when it comes to tolerance, there are books for that.

You don't go to bed with a book. Printed tits are only soiled paper; dissected "genital organs" are plumbing; whereas all medical imagery about sexuality calls to mind the gargoyles of Notre Dame. The hell of love as re-imagined by doctors has been purged of its Catholic monsters in favor of naturalistic fauna that includes embryos, prostates, uteruses, Fallopian tubes, "first spermatic emissions," fixations-regressions-perversions, gonococci, treponemes, spermatozoids that "discover mucus is a very favorable medium during ovulation," pubic symphyses, urethral meatuses, involutions of yellow bodies, papas barbus, soft chancres, condoms, tubes that become entangled and fat, gooey babies.

Of course, the physiological study of sexuality is necessary and fascinating; it can help to combat the superstitions, fears, ignorance that were kept alive by complete prohibition. But it's ridiculous for the biology of higher mammals to be passed off as an initiation to human sexuality. Because sexuality begins only when the organic machinery no longer limits desire, but submits to its randomness and favors its multiplicity.

This is what medical rationalism frequently denies: it describes our biological machinery, then it deduces from it a model of functioning; next it catalogues, under the name of deviances, all the sexual behaviors that contradict this mechanistic philosophy. But it dares not call deviant the crippled and hypersocialized sexual practices imposed by our morals. As a result, sexology ends up altering its descriptions to match what it wants to prove: ignoring or falsifying phenomena that aren't in agreement with the values that it defends; and continually mixing ideological vocabulary, moral assessments and scientific terminology into its conceptual tools.

Thus, it is neither an "accurate" nor a "human" science. Its official dissemination is a *repressive response* to the problem that suggests that contemporary society should recognize sexuality as a respectable sphere of freedom for all. Sexology observes the human body and claims to discover in it a universal truth about sexuality, in the name of which a rational order for the exercise of desire could be substituted for the old order. But, actually, this "truth" is not an endpoint of sex research: it is its premise. At the point of departure of its labors is a declaration of faith that maintains the existence and the permanent reality of a certain ideal "human nature," which will abide by the research that is carried out and the interpretation of the material that has been gathered. This postulate tries to reconcile the major humanist values of the exploitive middle class, the order of industrial society and the reformist spirit upon which its survival depends. On the other hand, as soon as the philosophical-political position of a sexologist is dissenting (and you'll see the same thing in psychoanalysis and psychiatry), his work suddenly accumulates the data, the conclusions that contradict established knowledge: we end up with a sexology of the left and a sexology of the right.[4] All that's missing, it seems, is a "revolutionary" sexology; perhaps because a scientific system of sexuality is being confused with the defense of a precise moral order, whereas dissenting thought has no model of order to propose, only forms of order to bring down; and where middle class knowledge sees commandments from "Nature," dissenting thought denounces the unspeakable laws that one part of humanity imposes upon the other.

Sexology manufactures a pyramid of sexual phenomena: the base is formed by biological data; and the tip is the adult and responsible subject, the scrupulous manager of instinctual capital—private property supervised by the State. All sexual behavior is, in fact, evaluated as *management techniques*, some aberrant (they squander instinctual capital), the others as commendable

---

4. A recent example of the latter: *The Erotic Function*, by Dr. G. Zwang—a monument to scientistic mania, false liberalism, café psychology and the erotology of the hospital staff room. Nevertheless, certain doctors have sung the author's praises for his "advanced" opinions about conjugal life. This doesn't prevent Dr. Zwang, starting with his preface, from admitting being a fanatic paternalist, double-fisted moralist, supporter of Western Progress, heterosexual with a hard one, guide and censor of humankind—and he goes to it with a furor that leaves far behind the fascism-in-good-taste to which old-fashioned sexology restricted itself. Note that Dr. Zwang is a "mad scientist"—because there's no longer anything scientific about him. Sexology is definitely the only modern discipline where—just because he is a doctor—somebody can "turn science upside down" to such a degree without anyone being shocked by or even conscious of it.

(they make the corporeality of the subject productive in an orthodox way). Sexuality is therefore understood as a function of a
single criterion: its profitability. In this way, sexology copies both
the values of middle class morality and those that serve to measure
the health of a capitalist enterprise.

This manner of assessment rejects the notion of costless
orgasms (and because it can't deny them, stigmatizes them morally),
and it reduces to fragments the phenomenon of sex on a global
scale. The study of sexology divides itself into isolated categories;
among them there is only a simple relationship of *value*, from the
inferior to the superior, a relationship that "justifies" a medicalized
theory of psychosomatic "development"—in love, marriage, procreation, well-accepted socio-sexual roles. The child's sexuality is
declared lowly and immature; it's opposed to the ossified mono-
sexuality of the normal adult; and between these two poles the
other kinds of behavior are distributed, from *least* to *most*, from bad
to good. The pyramid of phenomena is no more than a list of
winners. It's as if you were watching the win, place and show at the
races: there are the winning bets and the losing bets, the good and
the bad horses; the instinctual associations sanctioned by a certificate of civic-mindedness or health, and those which, disregarding
the finish line, roll around in the mud of the track or ramble
about—and the latter are monstrous, nobody's earning anything
from them and the society of exploitation could have kicked itself
as a result. The salaried guy who gets married at twenty-one and
shortly after has a child, a house and a car gets a gold star from the
sexologists; and like the schoolboy who succeeds at an arithmetic
problem, he can say: I passed.

Sexology would have us believe that its atomization of sexuality
is a response to a methodology. But since that method arises from

moral presuppositions, obscures the interpretation of phenomena, censors what produces them and denies what links them together, it is scientifically nonviable. The sex specialists, however, insist upon it, since changing their method would mean changing their ideology, which they don't want to do. From the hands of the moral Order, they receive an object of study that has been cut into slices and stacked hierarchically like the circles of Hell; sometimes they change the position of one or another of these slices (for example, masturbation has been "pushed up" and is becoming "good"), but they're very careful not to challenge the slicing-up itself. On the other hand, they increase the discriminations, the subtle differences, and infinitely fragment the data about the sexual experience. This tactic allows them to ignore in particular the socio-economic determinants of this experience and to allow psychological determinants only if they can submit to the biologism of the medical mind.

It's clear that sexology in its social aspect is the exercise of an abusive power. The discourse on sexuality is—even more than the discourse on mankind, art, civilization—the cultural privilege of the class in power. In France, the physicians' Conseil de l'Ordre, as we know, brings together members of the upper middle class who adhere openly to a conservative agenda, and who disown those practitioners whose professional behavior is dissident (for example, those who perform "illicit abortions" that are not very profitable, or spread sex information that is not very repressive). In our country, the institutional right to *talk sex* serves to crush a sexuality that has been condemned to silence. All scientific discourse that focuses exclusively on sex implies that the sex is censored. The medical source can lie, fake, falsify the knowledge that he dispenses as he pleases: because it isn't to his fellow citizens that he's accountable, but to the repression of the State.

In this way, the absence of a collective sexual discourse, of freedom of sexual practice, gets endorsed, and what's prohibited is intensified by sexuality being presented as a highly technical field, into which it's risky and forbidden to venture without a guide, and which the ignorant person can only approach after having subscribed to the abstract, regulated knowledge manufactured for his use—knowledge meaning, in this case, distance. Approach/avoidance: that is the very paradox of sex education.

As soon as the information ceases to be propagandist, economic and cultural frameworks restrict a large part of the access to it. The less reactionary it is, the less it becomes available as merchandise; you need to be cultured to understand it, persistent ("obsessed," in fact) to find it and "deviant" to criticize its weaknesses.

Here, as everywhere, information about it is distributed selectively; and the incapacity to judge it that results within the poorly informed silent majority is dubbed "freedom of opinion." The average citizen randomly manufactures his sexuality for himself with shreds of knowledge, the traumas of childhood, instinctual vestiges more or less well resewn together, and a neurotic selection of family taboos. Obliged to subject his sex life to social pressures that run contrary to it, he usually discovers only one solution: making a clean sweep, castration. Adult desire, whether it's "normal" or "perverted," has a mode of residual survival that is determined by a misunderstood and unnoticed exterior order. The search for a state of equilibrium in the context of desire, for the least suffering, the least frustration and a minimum of *ostracization* (either in relation to the behavior of the majority, or in relation to the codes of a "deviant" subculture) produces a sexuality that timorously obeys received patterns and aggressively imposes them on others. You have to respect the order so that it will respect you; and fight those who flout this great principle, or they could actually destroy the prison that protects you, steal the sexual rewards that you've learned how to obtain, depreciate the *actions* in which you've invested your libidinal capital in order to protect a fragment of it and sleep better at night.

The sex education of minors is accountable to the same process. Such cases begin with misappropriation, the deprivation of speech and corporality. We speak about sex to children and adolescents after having denied them all rights to sexuality. This "stolen sexuality" is restored to the minor in the form of a prescriptive and theoretical discourse. Sex as reinvented by this educational-scientific speech will play the same role as programming does in relation to an electronic device: it will dictate to the psyche the impulses and behaviors that exploitive society requires of us.

From then on, the minor will hear the voice of governmental sexology, he will be the spectator of another's sexuality, he will be *the voyeur of parental erotism.* He will remain without a sex, because society will only grant him one after fifteen to twenty years of brainwashing that only systematic frustration can render effective.

The child deprived of all social autonomy, of all spontaneous relationship to others, impaired, submissive, made to fall back on a father, a mother, the idiot box and a school that alienates, is given an "initiation" that informs him of the sexuality of big people and censors or ridicules his own eroticism. He is repeatedly told that desire is procreation, that prepubescence is impotence, that the practice of sex absolutely requires the possession of "operational" sex organs that allow intercourse between adults and impregnation. His urges are carefully socialized, he is "oedipalized," or, in other words, forced into a closed circuit of sexual economy that simultaneously harnesses his desire and prohibits it; and his mind is made to retrain desire into aggression, the search for pleasure into the acquisition of power, and erotic pleasure into owning objects.

The teenager—who is "free" to fool around a bit (if he is a bold and good-looking fellow) and to masturbate at night (if his family doesn't frequent too many priests)—is inflicted with an indoctrination designed to render plausible the prohibitions to which he continues to be subjected, now that he's the owner of that celebrated "potent" organism that prepubescence forced him to do without. But prolonging the frustration is indispensable: it creates the lust and blindness with which the frustrated person, once he reaches majority, throws himself into the sexual institutions that the State places gaping before him. A superior after having been a slave, new warder of female, childish or deviant humanity, he will be able to become that Father, owner and cop they'd promised he'd become if he first let himself be squashed for twenty years.

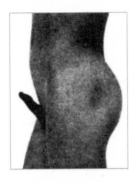

THIS IS WHERE HE WILL LEARN THE ROLE OF THE FATHER...

It seemed to us that the best way to help you respond to the child was to tell a "story," a story identical to yours...

This is where he will learn the role of the father, and especially, the existence of sexual relations, a special kind of relations that, to avoid being always an act of reproduction, quite often imply the love of a little future being.[5]

THE FIRST VOLUME OF the *Hachette Encyclopedia* is analogous to a lot of other works written for young children, and I wouldn't be interested in it if it hadn't marked the start of a gradual series of several additional books—a phenomenon that doesn't exist anywhere else.

Handbooks for "young people under 18"—socially asexual, at least in France—are the only form of sexual discourse to which they have official access: taken together, they represent all the sex that the child, the young teenager, has the right to openly possess.

---

5. Excerpt from the presentation sheet ("A Few Words to Parents") inserted in vol. 1 of the *Encyclopedia* (ages 7–9).

The works for ages 7–9 and those for ages 10–13 are completely interdependent. They are composed of a rather brief pseudonarrative and a very large set of illustrations that reduplicate it and accentuate certain sentences; they are the very opposite of decorative imagery and in many respects their psychological role is infinitely more important than the informative role of the text.

In this chapter, I will offer a few excerpts and descriptions of the age 7–9 volume, but I'm reserving the main part of my comments for the discussion of the age 10–13 volume. The period of existence covered by these two volumes is continuous, and it makes no sense to cut it into sections.

First, in the form of reasonably abridged excerpts (but with subheadings added by me), I present the essential passages of the little story that is told in the first volume—*a story just like yours…* I've only quoted physiological information if it was related to our sexual prohibitions; thus, these are the most daring of the disclosures in this first volume.

I. THE PLAIN AND SIMPLE STORY OF THE AVERAGE FRENCH PERSON

ONE FINE SUNDAY

This Sunday afternoon certainly is a promising one for Sophie and Thierry, seven-year-old twins: the whole family is going to tea at Aunt Nicole's [she's popping-out pregnant]. *She is letting them marvel at her pretty cradle in white and blue. Mom chats with Aunt Nicole. Dad and Uncle Jacques watch a soccer game on television.*
AFTER TV

"You said that Aunt Nicole's baby is in her stomach. How can that be? I don't get it." Dad comes over and sits the twins down in front of him. He must be getting ready to tell them a lot of things.

FOUNDING OF AN ENTERPRISE

Aunt Nicole and Uncle Jacques were both students, and some nights they went to the movies, to the theater or to concerts together. After their final exams, they went on vacation. Since they liked each other a lot, they often wanted to kiss. So much so that when September came they decided to live together and never leave each other. They moved into their lovely house, and Aunt Nicole was very happy. She'd tell herself that she could make a child happy. Uncle Jacques agreed. But how do you make a baby? I'm going to tell you.

PRODUCTION PLAN...

Babies are made, yes, made by the daddy and the mommy. To do this, they use certain parts of their bodies that are called the sex organs... the functioning of these organs can't be seen.

...AND EQUIPMENT

When a man is naked, you can see that he has hair at the bottom of his belly. Thierry, who is a little boy, doesn't have hair yet; but like men, like your dad, he already has a sack of skin that contains two balls called testicles, and a sort of tube, his penis, which he uses to pee. Pee is the only liquid that flows from a little boy's penis. From a man's penis, another liquid sometimes comes out, which never gets mixed with the pee.

The woman you see in the picture has her arms crossed over her breasts, it looks like she wants to hide them. At the base of her belly, she has hair, like the man, but no penis or testicles. In order to see her sex organs, we'd have to look inside her belly.

The opening of the vagina is found between the women's thighs, behind the hole she uses to pee.

STARTING MANUFACTURING

When one of these tiny sperms meets one of these tiny ova, they unite to form a baby.

The dad and mom have created a future little boy, or maybe a very pretty little girl! Kept nice and warm in this big pouch, the egg is going to develop.

DELIVERY OF THE PRODUCT

Aunt Nicole had understood that for the birth, she needed to be in shape. So she practiced. The mom must be calm, the delivery lasts a long time. Since she has done exercises to learn how to breathe quietly, she won't get out of breath. Look, the baby has come out! It's over, Mom will sleep now, with her baby close by.

INSTRUCTIONS FOR USE

A baby is incapable of coping on its own; he's cold; he's hungry. Since he soils himself, his parents will have to clean him and change his diapers. What a job, but also, what a pleasure! Thanks to this baby, the parents feel even closer to each other and love each other more.

POTTY CULTURE

Baby feels loved and protected. Soon, he'll realize that he has two hands. He loves being totally naked, wriggling and playing with his feet! A little later, Mom will ask him to go to the potty. He won't be very happy about it at first; but, to please Mom, he'll end up obeying her.

Soon, he realizes that he can stand like Dad and Mom. One day he walks all by himself. His parents praise him. But he's still small, he needs hugs. He's only happy when he's with Dad and Mom.

REINVESTMENT

His parents decide to take him to nursery school. He learns quickly how to live with other children. There are brunettes, blonds; some are very quiet, others uncontrollable. In general, the little boys are a bit stronger than the little girls.

A SINLESS PARADISE

Here are two happy children (image of a beach with no pollution and no crowds). *Last summer, you, too, liked being able to be on the* beach without any clothes on. Between two ballgames, the children ask questions, because some things seem difficult for them to understand. So they speak to their parents, who explain to them how babies come into the world.

ONE DAY, I'LL HAVE A "REAL" BODY

(Images: boy/girl after the onset of puberty). *The girl is admiring herself in front of the mirror. She has become tall and slender, her breasts have developed and she finds them very pretty. She's beginning to look more and more like Mom.*

The boy has body hair, too. Now he speaks with a low voice, almost like Dad. He's very proud of his shoulders, which are getting wider and wider, and his hips are narrow. He wants to look athletic.

... BUT I WON'T MISUSE IT.

Around 18 or 20, the teenagers have reached their adult height. Some of them are already beginning to work for a living. Others, if their parents can help, are getting their degrees. Boys and girls like to get together. They go out walking, to the movies, loan each other books and records.

THE ETERNAL RETURN

And then, like Aunt Nicole and Uncle Jacques, a boy and a girl realize that they like being alone together. When they're together, they talk, but they also get a lot of pleasure out of kissing. They will want to live together and will try to be even closer to each other; they'll be happy feeling and caressing each other's body.

WHERE THERE'S SMOKE THERE'S FIRE

One day they'll want to get married, they'll get even closer, the young man will put his penis in the vagina of the young woman, and they'll experience a new pleasure. Such pleasure is known as sexual pleasure. That's how you can—if you want to—have a baby.

II. LIST OF ILLUSTRATIONS

The book, which has 44 pages, includes 96 illustrations, 1 photo and 95 color drawings. The photo is on the cover; it shows a decent-looking naked little boy and little girl who are seated in an armchair and who are tanned and "good-looking"; the boy is holding the little girl by the neck and pretending to kiss her cheek. This pseudoflirting reminds us that children "are" asexual because they can only reproduce the parental stereotype as parody.

Here, arranged under simple headings, is the list of illustrations:[6]

Depictions of Naked Bodies
   Children: little boy-girl couple, 1.
   Adolescents: boy, 1; girl, 1.
   Adults: man, 2; woman, 2.

These drawings of nudes (which, aside from the child couple, are anthropometric in intention) are small in scale, simple and wholesome-looking. The genitals are invisible (women) or nominal (men).

Depictions of Sex Organs
   Images devoted to the "external genital organs": none.

Erotic Activity
   Depictions of any pleasure practice: none.

Reproduction
   Human biology: 3. Animal: 11. Plant : 4.

----

6. Three insignificant drawings aren't classifiable.

"Internal genital organs": 7.

Parental Couple: 8.

Intercourse for the purpose of procreation: 2 (Censored drawing, 1. Cutaway, 1.)

Pregnant woman: 20 (with internal views, 9).

Labor: 7.

Babies: 13.

Social Life of the Child
School: 1.

Family: 9.

Other situation: none.

For each, of course, I am referring to the main and explicit subject of the illustration.

It becomes apparent that, to an excessive degree, the accent is on procreation, with bizarre senses of propriety, unnecessarily daring touches (details of delivery, cesareans, etc.) and some peculiar omissions. I will get back to this. The eroticism of the child, like that of the adults, is absent from the illustration as it is from the text. By itself, the material on *pregnant women/birth/babies* represents 42% of the illustrations.

These illustrations are drawings because they are clearer and also less realistic than photos; their simple lines, their pastel colors tone down the subject being presented. My cataloguing of them doesn't give an account of an important piece of information: the relative size of the drawings. In fact, trivial, "emotional" kinds of illustration occupy the most space; by their themes, they seem intended to dupe girls rather than boys. I will come back to this point in the next chapter. Here, I'll content myself with describing the fourteen images that occupy either an entire page or at least two thirds of it.

1. *Family* smiling, in the street, in three couples: dad-mom, big brother-big sister, little brother-little sister. Dad in a suit, tie and pocket handkerchief; mom in a suit and scarf that hides her neck. "High-rise" style buildings on the left, car on the right, a little dog in front of it. The scene depicts a family unit on their Sunday outing: they are going to a relative's.

2. *Family*, at the home of the pregnant relative. She has a small dog to complement the one shown before (different sex, same breed).

3. *Couple*: love story in two images. On the left, a man and woman in proper-looking bathing suits, playing volleyball on a sunny beach. On the right, the same couple, but dressed, standing in the shade of a tree, smiling and looking as if they're about to kiss.

4. *Couple* with baby. In the first image, a young and happy mother, holding her baby against her body. On the right, an approving dog. In back, the husband smiling at them while painting a partition on wheels because he's furnishing their home: on the table, there's already a television, a model with a spherical design.

5. *Internal genital organs* of a man, seen in cutaway.

6. *Internal genital organs* of a woman, seen in cutaway.

7. *Ditto*, showing an egg.

8. *Couple*, two-page spread. Mom pregnant and lying on a bed in a private hospital. On the left, the dog and a designer suitcase. On the right, the husband leaning affectionately toward his young wife. In the foreground, her hand holding a sheet of paper and a pencil; on the sheet of paper you can read her ideas for a first name, in two columns: Antoine/Jean/Eric, Anne/Sophie/Isabelle. At the bottom of the image, two identical illustrations

depicting a baby in the uterus and reiterating the issue: girl on the left, boy on the right.

9. *Couple*, entering the maternity clinic. Taxi, trees, flowers, slender receptionist, pregnant woman. The man is holding her by the arm while clutching her hand; tall, healthy- and athletic-looking, he is carrying the designer suitcase.

10. *Labor*: finished. Mom on the bed looking happy, a young doctor to her left. On the right, a nurse dressed like a flight attendant is holding out the promised gift, I mean, the baby: of course, it's a boy.

11. *Mom* in a lovely negligee, with long, soft manicured hands, as in an advertisement for dishwashing liquid, is nursing her baby.

12. *School*: two boys, a girl, a table, goldfish in a bowl, educational games, pretty schoolteacher, little girls painting freely on a wall.

13. *Couple*: love story in six images. I: in the subway, a young man, standing, and a young woman, seated, are looking at one another, stiffly (man) or dreamily (woman). II: same people, at a dance hall, smiling at each other, dancing decently. III: same people, lying on the grass; they are dressed, smiling, arms around each other in a decent manner. The woman's position suggests controlled consenting-object; that is, leaning against the chest of the man, head under his, eyes raised, her arm supported by the man's hand. IV: same people, at a restaurant. Flowers, applauding, a toast going on behind them. V: same people, mating. The man is naked, lying on the woman, who is naked and flat on her back, all of this seen in profile. They are smiling like they were at the dance hall, their faces at a decent distance from one another. At the lower part of their bodies, the future of the species is being achieved decently, but we understand what's going on even so thanks to the cutaway view of VI: here the man becomes a blue silhouette with a protuberance, the woman a pink silhouette with a cavity containing the blue protuberance.

14. *Family* from the beginning. The lesson about things has born fruit; the couple hasn't had a fifth child, but there is a portrait of ancestors (grandma clinging to grandpa), a birdcage with two adult and four fledgling birds, the dog couple with five little ones—and, alone in its pot but radiant with duty accomplished, a cherry tree with its red cherries. I didn't count them.

Such is this first volume, reduced to what conveys its "scientific" message. The book has a very difficult role to play: it reveals "the existence of sexual relations" to human beings who have no right to them. First, two comments. The book, in terms of the level of its information, illustrations and narrative, is comparable to books published for children 7 to 8; but for those turning 9 or 10, it is excessively puerile. Because the book grants the latter only information created for seven-year-old readers, it is pedagogically backward, notably in comparison to very articulated textbooks meant for the same age bracket—but which, it is true, deal with material for which there is no moral necessity to prolong the infantilizing of those being taught.

The second comment is that the book pretends to initiate complete sexual ignoramuses, whereas no child could be considered to be one—except for the sons of priests, if that. The information is a combination of psychosocial propaganda and persnickety gynecology; it neglects the "sex life" and neuters physiology—not when such a thing is too blunt for children, but when it would seem indecent to parents. The book goes so far as to keep quiet about phenomena that are very familiar to the youngest of readers—erection, the genitals of little girls, masturbation, fondling, orgasms without ejaculation, for example—but that family education represses and makes them forget. The child has no sexuality in the eyes of parents, and that is why they're so unrelenting about it… It's extraordinary that the illustrations even avoid depicting a kiss, even though their characters are endowed with "good" biological prenatal impulses, which keep orality in its place in the hierarchy.

The child will understand that, outside of organs permitting him to be a father and wage-earner (a tall and muscular body, education, appropriate clothing, short hair, car, toolbox for fixing up the "lovely house," toothpaste smile, etc.), dad also has his baby-making tool. He has "what it takes" to uphold this father-role that society has given him, and to exercise his authority over wife and child, both of whom are precious objects and laughable subjects. This information invalidates the body of the child more completely than it had already been; and by describing to him what he can someday be, it orders him to conceal everything until then.

After this reading (repeated during three years of growth), children will be in no condition to make the slightest parallel between their prohibited sexuality and the activities that are depicted for them; they'll retain only one thing: *that there is no lifting of the prohibition unless you're an adult and you make a baby.* All the rest, even if it's subsequently explained and allowed, will be forever instilled with guilt—subjected to the first pattern of childhood, to that "primitive scene" of antisexual propaganda: and this is the sole effect sought by the education of little children.

Thus, the parents, because they are the exclusive agents of a reproductive process, have what it takes to obtain thrills and to exercise powers forbidden to children: "sexual pleasure", and especially, economic power, which many of the images stress in showing that the happiness of the couple is possessing and consuming. Nature, dogs, birds, cherry trees and parents determine the order for children/adults, which corresponds to a relationship among universal, reasonable and wholesome forces. I'm not capable of doing what my parents do, no one does anything but what my parents do, so I have nothing to do, except wait, while obeying them, to become like them.

In order to beautify(?) procreation, there's a mixture of biological facts and perfectly dubious socio-economic stereotypes—whose antiquated methods are, moreover, typical of a conservative, petit-bourgeois life style from the 50s—the golden age of this beautiful ideal. The couple is well matched, permanent and careful to represent themselves in a good light socially; they have the affectionate private ownership of the children with whom they have supplied themselves. The child's only existence is for this and because of it. All that he knows (family coercion, being shut up at home, the censure of his body, abusive discipline, an idiotic education, mind-destroying leisure activities) is his "natural" destiny, which began the day when the eyes of the man and the woman met in the subway. In a dignified way: since no matter how much one is "born of great pleasure," our parents did not get that idea groping tits and balls during rush hour; that would be too degrading for procreation. True pleasure is the reward for moral dignity and biological orthodoxy. Orgasm is a school principal's pat on the febrile head of the best student in the class.

When an ignorant child would ask his mother "where you buy babies," he was perceiving his real situation very well: being an object in a society where all objects are sold and bought. Thanks to sex education, he'll learn that family slaves aren't bought: they're "manufactured" by two of the people in your home. He, too, will make some later on: he's accumulating the losses for which to compensate, the frustrations, the grudges, the loneliness and the terrors; and while waiting, the toys, the teddy bears, the dolls, the playmates who are weaker are the ones who pay the charges. The "impotent" child chained to his family is already a very good reproducer of nonegalitarian order.

The imagery of married life, the family, education, in a dream-like atmosphere of ear-to-ear grins, indicates where to put one's energy in the search for pleasure.

For the child: a life in a bell jar, asexual affections, mothering of dolls or animals, a car you pedal, a cheerful school, castrating nudity—you can have a swim or play ball, but no fondling: on the contrary, if you notice that somebody has a body, you're supposed to go tell Dad quickly.

For the adults: being a happy consumer, having a well-defined, rigid social role, possessing a lot of up-to-date and expensive objects, being the most valued of them all ("very pretty breasts" or shoulders "getting wider and wider") and sometimes sampling the weird pleasure that comes with the act "that quite often implies the love of a little future being."

Thus, the absence of erotic depiction in the book isn't a negation of pleasure, but, rather, its wanton practice. The child is taught in which circumstances it should happen (intercourse-marriage),[7] why you do it (make a baby), at what age (in a very long time), according to which limit and with which vocabulary ("the young man will put his penis in the vagina of the girl" whom he'll have wooed in a decent way for a year or two), and finally, in which position (Dad on top of Mom, who's stretched out flat on her back, the only position that respects human law and the natural

---

7. The word itself is only written once, although the book implies it from beginning to end: "Do you know how Aunt Nicole and Uncle John knew each other before getting married?"

order, since "the little boys are" already "a bit stronger than the little girls.")

Obviously, if it were a matter not of indoctrinating but of informing, not of imprisoning but of liberating, we would have remembered that pleasure is the best way to make a child understand sexuality. It's the sole point in common that his body shares with that of the teenager, the very small or the adult—and also what makes girls identical to boys. But recognizing the erotic capacity of the child would redeem the reputation of uninhibited sexual expenditure, diminish the effectiveness of conditioning, ease the family's grip on the child, acknowledge his autonomy as a desiring subject, and shake two fundamental pillars of the sexual order: the duty to procreate, and parents' ownership rights over their products.

Let us marvel one last time at the legend of the baby-making couple, intended for the use of the children who've been had. That blissful and uncomplicated family subject to a just law; its new real estate, its new car, its new television and its vast brood; these little boys who never touch their pee-pee hose, and these little girls who have no sex organ at all; these easy, athletic, relaxing births where woman, in queenly motherhood and an elegant place like those where you have your nose retouched by a beautician, has just brought life into the world. In that society, there are no more poor or ugly, everyone is tall and thin, there are no more cripples or outlaws, inequalities or aggressions; you have children "if you want to" (but how not to want the "sexual pleasure" *that depends upon it?*); order is completely beautiful and everything under it and thanks to it is beautiful. You impregnate without getting hard, you come without moving; and just when you should, you "realize" that you "like being alone" with someone who—what luck!—also likes being with you. The only problem you have when it comes to understanding things is whether Antoine or Isabelle should be the name of the baby you'll raise in the very pretty house that you were able to buy when you had sensibly finished your studies.

This middle class Eden will be reduced to shreds by the "storm of puberty," as our doctors say. Cardboard pastorals will no longer be enough to conceal the real order; in the child who is growing, it will finally be necessary to recognize and better control this enemy of all exploitive order—an enemy that so easily becomes that order's corespondent and even its source: desire.

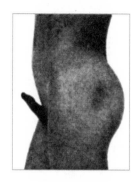

TO LIVE HAPPILY, LIVE CASTRATED

WHEN IT COMES TO information for minors, the *Hachette Encylo-pedia*'s volume for boys and girls ages 10 to 13 constitutes the most oppressive document that can be read on the current sorry state of adult sexuality.

This is why I have focused so much analysis on this unhoped-for material; the fact that the book is written for children certainly hasn't dissuaded me—especially since the final volumes (14–16, 17–18, adults) have nothing else to offer than a bigger forest for hiding the same trees—and what trees they are!

Neither can we neglect the contribution of "psychology" as a factor in the "success" of this particular genre, used as it is to dilute the batter, especially since this is the sole volume to benefit from it, thanks to the good offices of "Madame Claude Moran, psychotherapist." This sprinkling of outmoded psychoanalysis obviously has nothing that could embarrass the general reader: the transparent castrating tricks and rapturous "familyism" of the work reminds us, rather, what smug, elephantine and God-fearing psychotherapy is practiced on our shores by a great many kind ladies, in love with Papa Freud or at least with his penises—and to whom, each year, they sacrifice quite a few children, as Abraham wanted to do with his son for Yaweh, with the difference that neither angel nor demon would know how to stop them.

The introduction for parents to this book already contains the following wonders:

Sex information for the child of 10–13 creates a problem for whomever is responsible for him. Very many parents have in fact told us that he has apparently lost interest in things having to do with the body, with the great mysteries of life. The constant curiosity that he exhibited for everything having to do with reproduction and genitality has been repressed.

In reality, during the period that comes right before the storm of puberty, sexual desire is dulled or, rather, diluted by the discovery of authentic schoolwork and exciting first experiences in camaraderie.

… The dialogue between parents and child constitutes an excellent antidote against the repressive adjustments that come to light around the ages 5 to 6. Certainly, shame, a sense of decency, shyness are useful elements in the psycho-affective maturation of the individual. But, like all repressive systems, they must be counterbalanced, to prevent their soon taking on a tyrannical nature.

I wouldn't know how to better comment on these insanities than by paraphrasing them and moving from back to front.

Sex information for the child of 10 to 13 poses no problem for someone who has sex with him. Actually, very many children hide their interest in things having to do with the body from their family. The child no longer evidences any curiosity about the gynecological drivel of his parents: it's pleasure that interests him, exclusively, and he has learned that he'd better not brag about it.

In reality, during this period, his desire has been asserted, focused, and has assessed outside prohibitions. He is seeking to satisfy himself despite schoolwork, and frequently thanks to camaraderie and to his first experiences, which are secret if not exciting: jerking off, little magazines, dirty words, voyeurism, buggering, ladies' holes, etc.

The dialogue between parents and the child constitutes an insidious effort to reconsolidate the repressive adjustments that they've inflicted upon him from early childhood, and from which he's striving to free himself. Shame, a sense of decency, shyness help him a little to protect himself from parental aggression. His basic problem, in fact, is the immediate domination and the incessant control leveled on him by adults. The child of 10–13 thus has as much sexuality as he can, and if he has begun to carefully conceal it from those near him, it's often for the purpose of a lot of secret adventures, be they of any color.

No, I'm not claiming that "very many parents" have told me this, of course. I know it from the childhood of their children—and from mine and of the friends I had. At that age, whether or not you're having sex, you've understood that you can't recklessly exhibit your sexuality without risking losing it immediately—because parents, who are keeping an eye on their brats' puberty, are more curious and more indiscreet, more vigilant and hurtful than ever. Fortunately, we generally attribute an innocence to children, and this serves as the best protection for their "guilty" pleasures. The civil war between adults and their offspring is declared only at the time of the first growth of body hair, the first spurt of jism or first menstruation. Until then, a child who isn't too stupid or fearful, nor too much a prisoner of himself or others (which exists), can have an erotic life that is happier and richer than his parents'.

Among the majority of children, unfortunately, these ruses of desire hardly last: everything that has been put in place in the mind of the child continues to function, to come to a head, to devour his freedom and his life from the inside. This is because it's desire itself that feeds the self-repression of desire; soon puberty will give this self-repression an extraordinary strength, and the body ravaged by this policing "storm" will no longer be anything but a sad desiring vestige. The maturation of the body awards, in some way, a second organic life to a function that has been ransacked and mutilated for a long time and in every manner. And the glandular thrills causing the trembling in this little pile of libidinal ruins that is the adolescent will go straight to die right where it's been predicted that they would—in the latrines of preconjugal conditioning.

But let us remain, for a moment, on the "good" side of puberty. A child is supposed to be reading the volume whose introduction I have just quoted until the beginning of his fourteenth year. Sexual initiation takes place within the family. We see a dad, mom, their two children (an eleven-year-old son, nine-year-old daughter) and a pregnant relative—always used for display purposes. In the course of some "cheerful conversations," the parents answer the questions of the little ones—both more prepubescent than should be allowed, and who seriously risk setting 12-to-13-year-old readers' teeth on edge as they are forced to endure the inane company of these snot-nosed little brats made to measure.

And their horrible family: dad's an engineer, mom works as a data processor, the daughter, Sylvie, goes to school and the son, Jean, *is a fully developed high school student and happy about it...*[8]

_____

8. Unless otherwise indicated, the passages in italics are quotations from the volume commented upon.

Since Jean is a model child, with a model sister, model parents, a model home, a model mini-willy, model problems and a model relative, Juliette's the one who's oven-bunned.

The illustrations include 33 scientific drawings of small or medium format and 62 photographs, 94 pages in all. Here's the list.

DRAWINGS

I won't give details; they concern biology, anatomy, human physiology. In regard to good morals, I notice 1 penis in erection (cross-sectioned lengthwise) and 5 drawings devoted to contraception. No depiction of a vulva, even a schematic one.

PHOTOS

Depiction of Naked Bodies

We're dealing with a nudist family, so in the group photos there are lots of bodies. But these family nudes are nearly devoid of everything that characterizes nudity: you don't even see a pair of buttocks. I've listed those images under the heading "family" below.

Depiction of Sex

Images dedicated to "external genital organs":

—children: penises, 2 (one of which is in erection; this is the illustration that appears at the beginnings of my chapters, and it's also the smallest illustration in the whole book); vulva, 1.

—adults: none.

Erotic Activity

Images dedicated to any practice of pleasure: none. I have searched in vain for a trace of pleasure on the face of the individ-

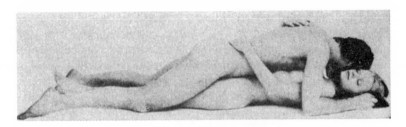

uals representing intercourse according to the canon in the work, and which I show here. What filthy things you have to do to have a kid... the couple seems to be saying. (These photos are classified further on.)

Reproduction
Biology: 4.
Parental couple: 4.
Intercourse for the purposes of procreation: 1 (previous page).
Pregnant women: 1 (with husband. Many other images in which she is not the main subject.)
Labor: 4.
Babies: 13.
Contraception: 1 (condom).

Social Life of the Child
The Family: 24. This abundance merits some detail; the large format of these photos, especially, calls for consideration:
—parents and children, 5 (4 of which are virtuous-looking "nudist" shots);
—brother-sister or cousin-cousin, 5 (one of which is a nude appearing on the cover);
—mother-daughter couple, 4 (naked without breasts, buttocks nor cunt);
—mother-son couple, 2 (dressed);
—father-daughter couple, 1 (dressed);
—twin-sister couple, 2;
—appearing as individual, 5 (idealized faces, full page. Girls, 4; boy, 1).

The outside world: 7. Interesting summing up of the extra-familial world: adults at work 2, children at leisure 2 (judo 1), environment 1 (high-rise building), third world 1 (starving children UNICEF style), sex life 1 (exhibitionist (*sic*) in a public garden).

As in volume 1 of the *Encyclopedia*, the accent is on the couple as breeders and the arrival of the baby in the family nest. But the insistence on family, source of harmony, protection and pleasure, is a lot greater. Here as there, no pictured reference to the eroticism of the child or the adult. The family-centric material (family, babies, parental couple, pregnant woman, labor) represents 50% of the illustrations.

The more null the informative role of the photographs, the larger they are. In full or double page, they essentially serve as counterbalances to the "subversive" effect of the disclosures to which, like it or not, a handbook of sex education is obliged. The authors have overexploited a well-known constant of the prepubescent mind: its interest in others and its exuberant affectivity (*we all need affection and tenderness, says Mom, pulling her big sulking boy against her*). That need for affection is what the photography excites, entices, gropes in corners and diverts to the proper place; it repeats to the young and frustrated that the family equals pleasure, that a mom is sweet, a dad strong, babies marvelous, childbirth a pleasure, modern life paradise, castration love, and that it does you good, does you good—have some more, it's homemade.

And whenever, for example, you are reading basic information about contraceptives, a baby's face, all of a sudden, appears in close-up—then, on page after page, come others, always larger, more touching, their eyes more animated, their cheeks rounder, adorable babies who tirelessly implore: please, *make me!*

Whoever's heart is not too hard and who compares these delightful little faces to the ghastly shot of the rubber that precedes them immediately understands which side happiness is on. Of course, preadolescents are more curious about the rubber than about babies: but they lose nothing by waiting, and their sisters are backing them up on that. Get that into your thick skull, it'll serve you well one day.

Besides, these behaviors are right in line with other propaganda—be it sexual or not—that the child has to endure. Television would be enough for it, on which those commercial breaks with a happy-family-eating-cauliflower-à-la-turd have, without any doubt, a greater power of indoctrination than sentimental songs and kisses about love-always.

Our family is on vacation here. In the morning, *Jean and Sylvie, with sand in their hair, salt at the corner of their lips, gulp down their café au lait in big swigs, like kittens who are about to be weaned. Their parents watch them, a little jealous of such appetite...* You've got to be a born mother through and through to write such phrases; and you wonder whether it's a question of someone touting a rising birthrate or a vapid incitement to pedophilia. *Living souls, you will see how alike they are* (Samuel Beckett).

The book is a kind of photo-roman, and the clichés that pepper its sentences are nothing next to those that illustrate them. These incredible, enormous photos, more doctored and more indecent than the covers of women's magazines, reveal to us the ways of a wholesome young-executive family that is "photogenic" to a nauseating degree. A socio-economic ideal through which the doctors sing their hymn to reproduction.

"*The reproduction of what?*" asks Sylvie.

"*Of the species, darling!*"

Dad is tall, muscular, dynamic, circumcised (it's cleaner); Mom is blond, thin and pretty; both of them are about as likeable and exciting as surgical instruments. Function demands it.

Beautiful children with long hair (they're "free") and simpleton eyes (they're "well-behaved"); Juliette languorously plump with her "little future being" (*You love him, even without knowing him?* asks Jean. "*I want him, understand,*" answers Juliette, *blushing a bit*), large garden, lawn, flowers, shrubs, hammock. You see everyone naked: when they are fashionable enough to be presentable, the family of today aren't afraid of their bodies. Anyway, seeing what's left of them, they would have no reason to be. The little boy? He's atrophied down there, and, in any case, the book coldly affirms for us that at his age you only get hard when you're sleeping. Mom hides her lovely pussy and her lovely tits behind her flat and barely slit little girl. As for dad, for a long time his paternal appendages reduced by conjugal duty haven't come to life for more than one night a week.

They shower, they touch (decently), they go swimming, run madly through the meadows, barefoot and hand in hand—an essential ritual when you have a second house and a good camera to immortalize such crazy happiness, such a "spontaneous snap-shot," which is staged before being canned. And then they talk about love, since they can't make it: biology, sexuality, chromo-somes, contraception, Freud, childbirth, you name it, and it happens, as long as every moment they can repeat babies, babies, babies... They say the word "jerk off" one time (*but I prefer,* says Dad, *using the accurate term: masturbate*) and even a pervert comes into the discussion (*Jean nods: "I saw one in the park!"*). A necessary audacity: because, in this ocean of well-being, you have to ward off the anxieties inspired by the other world—the one outside the book, outside the bell jar of designer families, the unclean world inhabited by the non-beautiful, the non-beautiful world where the non-rich live, the non-happy, the non-designer, the non-eunuchs, all the sick people.

It's interesting to compare this family to the large, no-frills traditional family from the preceding volume. With them, no one was a nudist; as often happens, the small children went nude on the beach, but their parents didn't imitate them. There was a large group of characters: eight people divided into four age brackets (grandparents, parents, teenagers, children), each forming an asexual couple (except for the parents). The beneficial effects of the parents were simple and concrete: caresses for the skin, food for the stomach, warmth and protection. This, moreover, created a meager image of the child and his needs: a little animal obsessed with organic and nutritive subjects, with a not very hard to please affectivity and an eroticism that was nonlocalized or null and satisfied by a bloated style of mothering; a stupid, selfish, prolonged baby, a douche-bag that you fondle and force feed—a subhuman who can barely move and speak.

Is that really what a child is? Certainly not, but it's what the family produces as breeder of meat and whittler-down of men. As a "producer" unit, it is in fact capable only of destroying the children that it turns out. And it pushes its savagery to the point of refusing them any contact, any influence that would repair that destruction and compensate for that mindlessness. For the great majority of parents, raising a child in their image is manufacturing a stillborn moron, a slobbering calf, a shifty slave or a cantankerous vixen. The tragedy of "reproduction" is already consummated when adolescents, finally provided with a critical tongue, begin to put their family into words—and to reject it, whereas unconsciously they'll belong to it forever.

The child of 10–13 is at the edge of that rebellion. The family imagined for him by the *Encyclopedia* is therefore infinitely more elaborated than the one meant for the little ones. The family he knows is a dumping ground of the wasted, the exploited, the dissatisfied that co-devours his life and tears his body, his mind, his desire to pieces. Yet it's depicted as a gilded cage that bestows well-being even to the neediest, and where the child is gelded merely to restore his sex to him, in chaste scenes of happiness through incest times four, and with the miraculous capital gain that comes from a good pro-life fine-tuning.

This is where he discovers the kind of home he can himself create one day, and in which conditions. He won't be clumsy and stupid like his parents: he'll be like that man or woman who is well-balanced, cultured, healthy, thin and functional. He won't lack money like his parents, he'll suffer no humiliations, unfairness, he won't be living on the bad side of exploitation: he'll have a "modern," distinguished profession, high earnings, an appearance beyond reproach, the socio-economic power to lead his own life and dominate others, like the couple in the book. He won't live in cramped conditions in a noisy, unattractive home: just like in the book he'll have a lovely house, a beautiful garden, space and calm. He won't have too many children, domestic quarrels, disgust with married life, relatives who are a pain in the neck: he'll found a liberated couple who'll lucidly examine its problems, and will beget the right amount of children that would be appropriate to the development of each and the number of places in a car. Unlike his parents, he won't be an exhausted, neurotic, bad-tempered, narrow-minded, duped, lackluster piece of human debris: he'll be the way they are in the book: an active, dynamic, responsible, well-adapted, well-informed adult. He despises the bourgeois conformism of today? The important thing is that he loves the one of tomorrow.

It would be better for him to forget his real family; he can even hate it, provided that he restructure his revolt into the wish to build an idyllic, bourgeois and proper family: this will be his revenge. This is how he is pressured into investing his desire in a family-centric project, while the realities that he does know are soothed away and those to which he will be open are pointed out—the most "beautiful" family imaginable. The family is bad and young people are discouraged from reproducing this monster? Fine. But nowadays we have Science and Freedom, gigantic gifts from Medicine and the State: so tomorrow's family will be a good one—a regular bargain to "take advantage of."

For centuries they've been cheating the gullible in this way: because tomorrow, things will change and pigs will fly, forget that today you're paying triple the price—and that tomorrow, like today, they'll pretend they're boring you to death, but you'll soon be squealing like a stuck pig.

All of this has no obvious relationship to "sex" education. However, the issue of sexuality is omnipresent—but, may I add, inverted. In this domain, it would seem indispensable to explain to the child, while it's not too late, what kinds of lies, blackmail and repressions have victimized him; to present the heterosexual couple and the family, with their morality and their passion for being the only ones to rule, as particular cases of sexual behavior and as historical absurdities from which knowledge ought to save us; to distinguish procreation as a minor possibility, a biological leftover of amorous activity—an accident, since that's what adults call unwanted births (almost all, according to them).

On the contrary, we start with Monsignor Baby, the only acceptable and "meaningful" aspect of the sex life, and will pitilessly describe each detail of his conception, gestation, coming into the world, mothering, libidinal fantasies. We refer to all the rest as if they were little secrets of cooking that are a bit embarrassing, but that certainly must be explained to the kitchen boy if you want him to do good work. We'll study the body because it's the headquarters for the production of babies; we'll approach pleasure as a curious byproduct of the act of procreation; and there will be no question of desire except through its conventions (preconjugal love story) or its alleged bad habits (oedipal mishap, masturbation, exhibitionism, sadists). The path of pleasure is strewn with thorns; desire itself is misfortune, defect, suffering, a terrible shadow that is a threat to the translucent delights of procreation. The family is the alpha and omega, all is subservient to it, everything that attains it is good, everything that steps away from it is bad.

"It's awfully well organized," murmurs Sylvie pensively.

If you say so, cutie.

Sexual initiation practices two kinds of misappropriation: linguistic and libidinal.

The linguistic misappropriation is very simple. The parents are the mouthpieces for medical knowledge; with precision they transmit the sexual lexicon that medicine has invented—and which is also a catalogue of organs that have no relationship to those with which the desiring subject is preoccupied:

"Show us the drawings," asks Jean. "Oh! How strange!"

"Look: here's an ovary."

For words from everyday language, this lexicon substitutes a scientific, indirect, convoluted and abstract vocabulary. For example, instead of the three terms, you get hard, you fuck, you come, here's how Dad explains it:

"Ejaculation is a spurt powerful enough for a sperm to reach the ovum (sic, strictly). *The man has inserted his penis into the vagina of the woman. Of course, in order to be able to enter it, his penis must have an erection, or in other words, be hard." Dad looks at his son and smilingly adds, "You must have heard the word* hard-on, *that's slang but it means the same thing..."*

"But, Dad, what makes the penis get an erection? When I wake up in the morning, sometimes I have an erection, but the rest of the time it's completely limp..."

This is how we get to a gratuitous kind of technical language about the knowledge of sexuality, in which the simple, familiar word is only "slang," or in other words, subjective, extrafamilial, unscientific language, incapable of naming. Understanding what makes the word "masturbate" "accurate" as a way of talking about jerking off is to discover how middle class medicine contrasts the language of its own class with popular language about sexuality, a language that is shocking because it eroticizes the phenomena being referred to, whereas scientific language freezes it. In the same way, we also have "accurate" sexualities (fittingly medico-genital) and "inaccurate" sexualities (hedonistic, selfish, vulgar, perverse, etc.). Medical language affords sexuality a decency that allows it to be introduced, properly lubricated, into the conduit of middle class talk.

Moreover, a sexual initiation can't be done within the family and in slang at the same time. Slang is the secret language adopted by desire to express itself in the face of repression, whereas the family is the first of the repressive authorities. Sex education exists to prevent the acts, to hinder and position them. The child is perfectly aware of the prohibitions he's enduring; he knows very well why he knows nothing, and whose fault it is. He'll sense that the sex education information being dispensed by his parents or the school, far from allaying his frustrations, is burrowing into them, rummaging through them, checking them, watering them down, setting up a system of language in them that will end up estranging his desire.

Compelling the child to say "my penis is getting an erection" instead of "my cock is getting hard" is dispossessing him of his sex, transforming an intimate, pleasant occurrence, which carries its share of embarrassment, pleasure and expectation into an anonymous, strange phenomenon, subject to a medical explanation that recuperates it and invalidates it.

But if Dad, like friends in class, said "cock" to his son, a kind of incestuous violation would be added to the linguistic violation. In fact, in a sexual initiation tacked by the parents onto the frustration that they are inflicting upon the children, all the words sound false, too near or too far away, always prying and always repressive—because these are the castrators who are saying them.

Undoubtedly, the child would be more sensitive to such aggression if Dad would use familiar language. Instead we stay suavely medical and won't pronounce obscene words except in the case of certain delicate open-heart operations. In the work I'm discussing, the father only resorts to them three times: get hard, jerk off, have sex. These are words that, we are told, his children know; as secrets, they create an embryonic private life for them. Therefore, their appeal must be defused and the libidinal void must be re-established (you've got those words for hiding your desire, I'm taking them back); we must rout these pretty serpents from their hole and slap over them a lousy Latin word that stigmatizes them. Gliding from scientific heights to slimy familiarities, Dad castrates, castrates and castrates; the information on sexuality that he so generously deals out comes down to a loathsome expurgation of the desire that is brewing and growing in secret in his children.

In the end, we see that if Dad says "jerk off" is "inaccurate" and "masturbate" is "accurate," it's because the first verb is party to the thing, and it's "inaccurate" for it to merit being party to it; whereas "masturbate" is a cold, lame, off-putting verb that makes the word being referred to appear ugly—therefore it alone is "accurate." When you jerk off, you do something whose real name I know: here it is, the thing that will make public the filthiness of the pleasures in which you indulge.

Misappropriation goes even further when the scientific discourse downright misrepresents the given data. Examples abound page after page with the sexologists, who handle all the subtle falsification like master quacks. Here, specifically, is the part following the passage I was citing, concerning erection:

"...completely limp..."

"Because you're still too young! At your age, erections come during sleep. But you can also be excited by a strenuous game, sports, or even a feeling that brings you pleasure. With adults, it's desire that causes an erection."

I wonder what all the boys will think of that explanation who at eight as at thirteen have the depravity to get hard while awake and do it on purpose; whose fingers are quite familiar with the "strenuous game" and the "feeling" that "brings pleasure." Will they be worried about being abnormal? Will they be proud of it?

But why this big fat medical lie? Obviously, there are boys who are so castrated that they are like little Jean, completely surprised when their pee-pee sticks up, incapable of seeing the cause of it, (if there is one—"involuntary" erections are neither more nor less frequent with adults than they are with children), boys who become wide-eyed if someone explains to them that with adults it's because of "desire." What dat? In principal, the book postulates that children have no idea of it, and it sinks into a ridiculous dialogue (but one that, I'm sure, will soften up the mothers in the family):

...it's desire that causes an erection. The desire for someone else."

"The desire for someone else? As if you wanted to eat them?"

Mom bursts out laughing. "Now aren't you the big eaters! But that's not altogether wrong... Desire is like a kind of craving and even like appetite. When you want a piece of cake, your "mouth waters." When a man and a woman look at each other with pleasure, desire one another, want to unite intimately, certain physical changes happen that prepare their bodies for that union."

"But..." sighs Jean, "isn't desire love? In movies, on television, when lovers kiss, they're thinking of cake?"

"Mom was just giving an example, big fella! If I'm cuddling with Mom, I'm also desiring her, but that has nothing to do with wanting some pastry! I'm also moved, filled with tenderness, I need to caress her."

"And that gives you pleasure?"

"Yes. Desire's part of love. Men and women love to unite and not only with the hope of having a child."

"And animals?"

This wonderful passage clarifies for us the motives for the lie that I was pointing out. If the authors are committing it—even if they are addressing readers who are in the best position to detect it—what they want, at any price, is to disqualify the sexuality of the prepubescent child. They've depicted the erection as the necessary and satisfactory condition for intercourse—and yet the child gets hard, too, unfortunately. The only way to put him back in his place is to destroy that erection with casuistry.

Consequently, the child won't "really" get hard, it's involuntary, anything at all can stiffen his prick, except desire, the real thing, that remarkable "desire for someone else" that leads straight to the marriage bedroom. Does the boy have sex organs? Why no, it only looks like it, he has nothing at all, it's only hot air, he doesn't even know what to do with it.

The child is actually kept in such ignorance and at such a distance from his genitals that he can get hard without dreaming of taking the least advantage of it; it's what's left, like a monument still standing in a city razed by war. Once emptiness has been created in the mind of the child and around his body, for him his penis becomes an instrument that's out of order, and for good reason.

But this "perfect" castration is far from being the rule. First of all, the family—I'll explain this later—symbolically makes use of the child's sex. Next, it's false that the erections of a lot of prepubescent boys are involuntary, uncontrollable, incomprehensible, "passive." False that they don't know desire, desire for a person or desire for pleasure. False, finally and especially, that a child's right to an erotic life must increase in relation to his ability to make love exactly like dad-mom. His body isn't the same as theirs, nor is his penis; his mind isn't the same as theirs; his amorous needs are his own. Incapable of procreation and relatively incapable of orthodox coitus with an adult according to the model of matrimonial, puritanical fornication, he's nonetheless prepared for pleasure, a creature (as all parents and all doctors know) in whom desire awoke at the same time that he opened his eyes, that his body touched its first objects and received its first pleasures. Whether it's deliberate or unconscious, family repression forces him to unlearn what no one without such repression would ever have the need to relearn at a later time.

The doctors will be proud of how liberal they are: they've dared to talk about erections, desire, intercourse, contraception to people less than fourteen years old. Yes, but that daring gesture—which waited for authorization from the State before expressing itself—is a chance for them to spread the most narrow-minded sexual morality, the most hackneyed commonplaces of petit-bourgeois coitus (desire like an "appetite" and that "is a part of love," the "tenderness" that Dad is going to prove to Mom, the "cuddling" that he slips her to announce that he wants to get off). They even add that you "don't just" make nookie to procreate, but they reserve that pleasure for the big people and pass quickly to something else ("And animals?"); and they certainly don't admit that men and women fuck in perpetual fear—and not "with the hope"—of having a child. They celebrate pleasure without restrictions provided that these only depict conjugal pleasures (fucking "Mom") and reject those that make up the entire sexuality of the child and the disinterested pleasures of the adult.

You have to be a cynic and profoundly dishonest to call "innocence" (as religious zealots say) or "polymorphous perversion" (as psychoanalysts say) the dissymmetry that exists between the child's sexuality and that of the adult who has been brought to heel. The latter is conceptualized, hypercoded, socialized and sermonized in excess, thinks about itself, is of two minds, assesses itself, polices itself, weighs and counts its expenditures, its roles, its appearances, its winnings and its assets. A child's desire doesn't conform to such parochial management; multiple and nameless, running everywhere, searching for everything, kissing everything, open and shut, grasping and wasteful, selfish and infinitely generous, all he can see in adult sexuality is an exotic, grim, incomprehensible and vaguely unsavory fable, like the entire world of parents—its thrift, etiquettes, prisons, borders, sexual and affective baseness.

But the child smothered by these corporal prohibitions, crushed by parental models, repudiated even in his desire (you want to come? eat some cake, at your age it's the same thing), forced to precociously reproduce the flaws, paralyses, mutilations of the adult world, is in a weak position: he's someone permanently under siege who, except for a very uncommon stroke of fortune, forgets himself, surrenders, becomes lost and gives in to the strongest. This is the price of his survival. Suddenly he is helpless, asexual, non-desiring, impatient for us to teach him our miserable sexuality after having stubbed out the brilliance of his—a brilliance that isn't part of being a "child" but the feature of every man, before the order brings him down. This is the defeated child that the doctors show us with satisfaction—passive, constricted flesh ready to flow into the mould that Dad and Mom cobbled together for him under the watchful eyes of the State.

Truth is fine, but the order is better: the former engenders freedoms that the latter condemns. It's not difficult to imagine which side will win out. So we'll tell children that they're not mature enough physically to have a sex; and when they become physically mature we'll tell them that they're not yet psychically up to par. This is the way we pull a donkey along by a carrot until the age of about twenty, and sometimes more.

Sex information has been provided through the expedient of a family story so that family and sexuality seem ineluctably implied by each other. Sex education teaches that a family doesn't come into the world with the help of the stork but between two bed sheets: and that's what sex is for, and only for that. Even if it means that the parents have a right to a "premium on pleasure," once they've accomplished their task as breeders. Similarly, the liberal-ization of morals and contraception will be a "premium on well-being" awarded every obedient home: they won't be a way of freeing the individual from the sexual or social prisons in which the State wants him to hide himself away.

Thus, the little heroes of the two family books (7–9 years, 10–13 years) will have only one big question to ask: how babies are born. A concern that will be timidly overtaken by another in the second volume: how do adults have sex? On the other hand, the children will never ask: why don't I have the right to touch my body and others'? Why am I shut up here? Why do you have sex and I don't, although I can and want to? Why do you speak to me as if I were blind, powerless, an idiot? Why have you made so many little mysteries, and are you taking advantage of them now, to tell me what's convenient for you and not the truth? Why show me these organs, these glands, these innards, these fetuses, and prevent me from freely seeing the outsides of bodies?

Such a list of contradictions could go on to infinity. Of course, as soon as Dad and Mom have to clear up the mysteries that their own censure has created, they rush around with the task of making them seem completely natural, innocent and nameable without defying morality. But if this is the case, why are morals so rigid that another vocabulary would be in defiance of them? Why are parents, doctors, educators in league to prevent the child from experiencing what they claim to be teaching him? Why this absolute silence before this mountain of "revelations"? Why these pregnancies and these deliveries, images as painful for the child as they are for the adult (even women don't get to see their own delivery from this perspective, it's a sight reserved for the attending physician)? Why these lies by omission whenever "nature" offends morality? Why are these caresses and this desire recalled so obscurely whereas desire and caresses are what have bound the child to his family circle since the time he was born?

No answer for that. But we understand that the book is portraying questioners between the ages of 9 and 11: their excessive naiveté will stay almost unnoticed, and they won't ask any more about it than can be said. The older readers or less inane ones will have to restrict themselves to the same limits. If they think they're swindled, infantilized, ignored by the work, "Jean and Sylvie" will prove to them that they're wrong. The doctors are building an official model of the child 10–13, a falsified model but one that supports the authority of scientific knowledge and that is approved by the parents. The real children will know what they must be like sexually to be accepted. Each reader in his own corner, with his bizarre excess of sexuality in relationship to the model, will think he's unique, exceptional, vaguely abnormal, and will stifle his desire. He won't know that most children have the same "anomaly" and that the wonderful child-of-the-doctors is either a victim or an imposter. He'll suffer from his frustration and feel the desires that cause it: he'll fight them, conceal them, admit them timorously to get help, or he'll satisfy them shamefully. Such mortification was invented by Christianity; medicine takes it over, and the order goes on.

The eroticism experienced by the child, which the book silences or defiles, will be permanently linked with guilt: now, all sex is bad, except within family nuptials, which alone have been absolved by medicine. *We'll never be afraid of ourselves, later on?* ask the two simpletons at the end of the manual. *For one thing, you won't be ashamed of your body, and you won't be afraid of being punished for sexual desires,* answer the parents, who had first remarked: *too many people aren't aware of how their whole body functions, so how could they be balanced?* We can marvel at the fact that human-ity was able to live for such a long time, to prosper, reproduce, invent, rule, be cheerful sometimes, when there was no sexology to teach it the right path to happiness. It's true that our ancestors were "unbalanced": they fucked in every kind of position, wore their hair long, hardly ever washed except for pleasure, felt each other up, fornicated without hiding it, sucked and ass-fucked each other, walked on bellies to cause abortion, had orgasms far and wide, without consideration for age or sex—as is attested by today's sciences concerning prehistory, antiquity, primitive cultures and, indirectly, animal biology itself. Nature's aberrations, which bour-geois society has rectified: years ago, the Puritans of America demanded that domestic animals—dogs or horses—wear boxer shorts in public to hide their private parts; and modern medicine, for its part, finally possesses the secret of sexual balance. It's in knowing what it knows (a necessity that no one contests, even though no one thinks it's enough); but also, and especially, in believing what it believes, doing what it says, hating what it con-demns, deciphering ovaries and balls like it does, where the moral Law of this little half-century in a little country of the West is miraculously found written. If knowing "how the body functions" is all we need to be "balanced," it's because sexology, more fortu-nate than Claude Bernard looking for the soul under his scalpel, has discovered, by means of dissections, the basis of good morals: and obeying them is the requirement of that balance. The text of the *Encyclopedia* is clear, explicit and implacable when it comes to that. What represents crime or delinquency for middle class laws, scandal for middle class morality, sin for middle class religion, is deviance, imbalance and disease for objective medicine and has no politics for the bourgeoisie in power.

It's useless to fight for sexual freedom: liberty is virtue. Modern children will no longer be "ashamed of their bodies" (were they ever, unless it was taught by their parents?): we've merely made them ashamed of the bodies of others. They won't be afraid of being "punished for sexual desires"—in so much as no law is punishing them, really: only pleasures are punished. Pleasures of the child, of every minor, of the unmarried, of women who no longer want to be slaves, and of perverts; in short, around three quarters of humanity. And fine people have a way of tormenting and excluding—in a way that is more ruthless than any executioner, any exile—those delinquents whom contemporary Justice is lenient enough to absolve. This moral lynching is even the most ordinary kind of sensuality about which the mild-mannered morons of our land agree.

Obviously, the guilt-mongering of pleasure will no longer be enough to hold back the teenager; but underlying his disorders, well anchored in his desire, which is becoming blatant as it lives its last hours, it will leave its mark upon the long, hard and grueling adult age to follow, during which all the lessons of childhood will reawaken one by one and lock the fellow in the dungeon built for him. It's like an order slow on the uptake, or a poison whose greatest effect is produced a very long time after it's been administered, even if you've forgotten all about receiving it a long time ago.

In the meantime, it will have been invaluable for preadolescents to remain subjugated to the world of the "little ones"—just like they remained among the Mothers before, until the moment when their development became too obvious and the society of the Fathers took charge of them.

Here is the only description of the act of love meant for those less than fourteen. It's altogether worthy of those photos I reproduced, with the two sulking wet blankets used to glorify conjugal love:

"Look at the photo," says Dad. "The man lies on top of the woman. He puts his penis in her vagina. It's easy because the vagina has become very moist and his member slips inside instinctively. Their two bodies become no more than one. The pleasure that both of them are feeling becomes so strong that the man has an ejaculation. This is known as orgasm.

"Do you have to move? I mean is it enough just to stick your penis in?" says an attentive Jean.

"The man and the woman find a movement together—one that's in tune with their bodies. They kiss 'on the mouth,' too, like you've already seen in films."

"With their mouths open? Touching tongues?"

"Yes."

"And afterward? If the penis runs out of sperm, does it become limp again?" says Jean.

"Yes. Desire stops exciting it after a certain time. The man and the woman are happy, calm, relaxed. They feel wonderfully peaceful together."

Must I, yet again, insist on the fact that this "scientific" description of a "natural" act is actually the announcement of a Puritan protocol for coitus, bowdlerized and socially coded to the teeth? The man "lies on top of the woman," "easy" and "instinctive" penetration, desire that "excites the penis" if the latter "has some sperm," a couple that now forms only one body, and this final irony: all these lurches to produce... the man's ejaculation. No female orgasm? No, Mom silently plays the mattress and appreciates "orgasm" behind the scenes. *It's the sperm that runs the show*, as Jean says in another place.

Mysterious rite from an unknown land, coitus as an instinctual machine during which one "has" an ejaculation. The pro-birth, paternalist and puritan stereotype seems so estranged from the human body that you're no longer even certain that it's participating in the affair: *Do you have to move?* asks Jean, who has probably never churned his loins against his sheets, rubbed his stomach against a friend or his sister while he was pretending to fight, or wanked his butt against the seat of his bike while playing the champion.

This great moment of "instinct" is a restrictive socio-cultural model that dad-mom hands down, a recipe for good sex that allows you to pull through at the least expense. What is it "enough" to do in order for it to function? Disappointment: no matter how much you take the right position, close your eyes, kiss like in the movies, squeeze your buttocks together like at church, imitate your parents, put your cock in the "moist" oven, and wait for it to heat up "so strong" that it overflows, nothing happens; you "have" to see to it, the "instinctive" mechanism is imperfect, you must—horror or horrors—be there.

Fortunately, the fact that they're two of you gives you the guts, you get rid of the blunders, you "find together" the movement that makes it easier and quickly produces the mini-frenzy, the little binge, the little death in which the mind, overtaxed by the obscenities that you inflict upon it, finally gives up ground—after having verified that everything took place as prescribed and that you didn't mistake the hole, the position, the role or the gestures. Consciousness resurfaces once the danger is past, during the time of feeling "wonderfully peaceful" that follows that vile abuse that Nature commands us to do and from which Nature claims its fine fruits. A duty, in truth, that would exceed the force of morality for normal citizens if this model of decent coitus didn't exist—wasn't universally taught, if not practiced, since there has been a Christian god—and didn't at least put the worst stains of the "sexual relationship" under cover. Obviously, it's always easy to put the blame on Nature's back, and that very sad beast with two backs plays a bit part.

You listen to your friends at school who often will say anything at all! says Dad. You certainly won't risk being swallowed up by the bad habits of desire after having listened to him. Doesn't he add that he's describing that act *so that the birth of a child stops being the great mystery for you*? He certainly can disclose the "pleasure" of "uniting intimately" since there's a baby brewing. Also, when the narrative boldly adds that, after having made love, Dad and Mom *sometimes have a renewed desire for each other and make love several times*, the children immediately disregard that trifling detail and ask the real question that is on their mind:

"And when can a sperm come together with the ovum?" inquired Sylvie.

And how to prevent them from coming together, at the right time? When it comes to contraception, the book displays a rare aptitude: the usual procedures have barely been enumerated and the pill mentioned when the child, remote-controlled by our authors, has a new worry:

"The pill, does the pope have something against it?"

"Some religions forbid indulging in sexual pleasure if you don't want to have children. The pleasure itself is often considered to be a sin... The pope has come out against using the pill."

"So do women obey him?"

"Some women respect that ban."

Oh, "some women," who don't obey (how low) but who respect (how worthy), humanity admires you! And here is plainly all that this work has in store for the moral—and political—issue continually posed among us by contraception. It's quick and well done. The show of "objectivity" lets the authors avoid giving their own opinion; they're content with reporting the pope's, but none other; and the position of respectful women, but none other. And there you have it.

It's strange that this passage—each word of which has been carefully weighed—borrows the prohibition against fucking when it isn't to cause pregnancy from "some religions." What other religion except Christianity, in fact—our own religion, the one that manufactures our morals, our science, our doctors—has advocated that prohibition, and still does? It hasn't dared to do this openly for ages, moreover, and is satisfied with condemning the effective means of contraception while approving of others—which comes down to encouraging secret innovation, jerking off, coitus interruptus, rubbers, adultery, coming to an understanding with the confessor and knitting needles. But by attributing to religious morality an attitude that's more repressive than is true, conservative doctors paint themselves up a good fall guy and give themselves a great air of freedom and reason, since—height of tolerance—they say that a married couple has the right to have sex without producing children—especially if they have some already.

The paragraphs on contraception, posed in such a way (and I've told how they are cleverly paralleled by pretty full-page photos of babies) certainly weren't difficult to draft. All the more so since contraceptives are useless to children and access to them impossible for minors, including those who reach the age of needing them (a small detail that the book, in its elation over modern "freedoms," obviously doesn't mention). All that remained was a contradiction between the pro-birth perspective of the work and that daring information whose absence would have caused a scandal. The problem is poorly resolved: contraceptives, we're allowed to understand, are intended for families that are becoming too large. This small breach in the inevitability of biology will therefore not represent an opportunity for an escape from the conjugal setting: it will work to give a little breathing space to the prisoners found there, who mustn't leave under any pretext. More worthwhile, Jean realizes himself, to have *six* children you can feed rather than *twelve* weighing you down. This magnanimous opinion gives the "France of one hundred million French" a fair opportunity to go into labor soon.

There's a joke that Grandmother will tell you, too, the mom says all of a sudden to her little girl. She wants to talk about the results of the Ogino, or Rhythm, Method tolerated by the pope because it fails—a "contraceptive" procedure that has probably led to the birth of half of our parents and ourselves. This will be the theme of a delightful joke, as if this disgrace, which is responsible everywhere it's used for so many unwanted children, ruined couples, savage abortions, were a joyous prank by the Church on Christians, who are delighted by papal humor:

"They're surprise-babies!" guffaws Sylvie.

Thank God that there is at least a respectable tragedy, a terrible one; Dad describes *it in a more serious voice: there are couples who passionately want to have a child, and who can't.*

"They can't?" repeats Jean, dumbfounded.

This time no one "guffaws"; the problem is too "serious"—even if there is a frequent and well-tolerated solution, adoption. And it doesn't get rid of the misfortune of not being the "natural" owner of a piece of flesh that has come out of your own womb, a property and yield that has been depicted to men and women as the greatest of necessities and the best emergency exit, in view of the setbacks of married life and individual failures. Stubbornly, women repeat that their marriage is a catastrophe and that their private or social life is pitiful; stubbornly, doctors, moralists and hack journalists retort: have a child, it's the remedy for everything. You can guess, as well, what family life will be for these child-remedies, these life preservers clung to by so many swindled women, selfish people, specters, slaves and imbeciles—as if the only way to finally know L'AMOUR!, without concession, were to manufacture your lover yourself. In any case, whoever is deprived of such a course will truly be able to feel disabled, frustrated, victim of an unfair fate. Looked at this way, adopting a child won't be enough to achieve a good capitalist, family-centric recompense: doesn't medicine say over and over that motherhood is indispensable to the full development of a woman? Lay an egg, unattractive girls, and you'll finally become desirable, sweet, pretty, happy, protected and respected. The other side of that propaganda, I'm afraid, is that there are sterile women and barren couples. In this case, doctors can no longer do anything but get out their handkerchiefs, wear mourning and rub onion in their eyes: hmm, isn't Nature cruel—giving us organs for making babies that don't work! Then what's left of life? Living? To do what? Have pleasure? Without a baby after? That's too hard to accept. Adopt abandoned babies? Other people's? Who knows what hole they crawled out of, these depraved women, heredity and all that? Picking up that kind of a throwaway, taking such a risk, undergoing such humiliation? It's mind-boggling, sure is. From the good joke about the unwanted brats to the great tragedy of being unable to have kids, *a lot of problems come up, then? Before and after birth?* remarks Sylvie, breaking into *a big sigh*—and, essentially, rendering children themselves guilty of the defects in the social order. It's because of your love for us that you'll suffer, dads and moms, we really owe you a lot of gratitude. Nature, a good fairy that watches over cradles, suddenly becomes a cruel stepmother, as soon as we leave the gilded world of the propagandists and touch upon a few realities of the "sex" life.

Therein lies the great absurdity of the subsequent volumes of the *Encyclopedia*, which will be compelled to tell more about the sufferings, difficulties, failures, utopian views of the sexual order, and to say less about its virtues—without casting any doubt upon it for a single moment. The family paradise in the volumes for children will be revealed to be a hell, a place of every hardship where you're supposed to be happy anyway. Nature, Instinct and their commandments will no longer come true "easily," but at the price of such a quantity of formulas, precautions, resignations, controls, warnings, submissions and learning, that the equilibrium of this good sexuality will seem like a cruel exercise in acrobatics at the edge of the impossible—and its miraculous happiness, a terrible ecstasy, which, on the photos of tormented victims, pacifies the faces of those who have been tortured too long. The hedonists and deviants and the perverts whose sexuality, unforeseen by biology, dismembered by medicine and persecuted by laws, remain standing alone and on every front, will be denounced with hate; whereas good, "natural" sex, taught to everyone, favored by the order, fawned upon, validated, consoled and blessed, bought for men with volleys of benefits, indulgences, reductions in taxes and obscene or virtuous gadgets to smarten it up, will be nothing but a house of cards that collapses with the least puff of air whose ruins medicine, religion and police strive in vain to prop up.

Be that as it may, the genuine usefulness of contraceptives is clearly delimited by the book: they're for Indians who are too fertile, starving Negroes, all the poor. On one side we have our societies of abundance and their privileged families who raise a number of children without strong material hardship and keep them on a tight leash; and on the other, the underdeveloped countries, meaning the ransacked ones, where the populations, deprived of the essentials and divested of their resources for our profit, are requested to reproduce a little less, or else this lovely system of connected vessels is in danger of having some disturbing hiccups.

Now that the problem with contraception has been wedged between the good pope and the wicked third world, we can return to serious things: the Western family, children, desire and shame. This is the agenda of the Hachette collection: *from physiology to psychology*. A strange kind of physiology, as we've understood. The psychology is quite something, as well.

I wonder why our authors have insisted on endowing their little heroes with so much embarrassment, guilt. They must have thought that since this guilt existed, the text needed to show it; but that's plunging their model characters into the very attitudes that sex education is supposed to put an end to. Following are some examples, presented pell-mell:

"Below it (the penis) I've got something else, a sort of little sack," says the little boy, mustering his courage...

"Oh yes, periods." (Sylvie fidgets a little on her chair.)

"Don't be embarrassed, darling."

"... we really don't dare to talk to you about it!" Sylvie stares down into her cup.

Jean gives a little cough, then says in a low voice, "Dad never explained how you make a child..." Sylvie, overcome, jumps into the water. She's blushing like one of those fresh, sweet tomatoes from the Saturday market. "What does it mean: have sex?"

The two children raise their eyes toward Dad and Mom, whose eyelashes have fluttered imperceptibly.

"You're brave," says Dad…

It will take a lot of courage, certainly, for real children to follow the example of Jean and Sylvie, stick their head into the lion's
mouth, fling everything they've preserved about sexuality between
the clutches of their parents, just so it can be mangled under the
pretext of informing them. It will be the big day of admissions, a
settling of scores; you will be, boys and girls, stripped bare, exhibited, hoisted onto the operating table and flayed; and as for that
veil of silence that covered sexuality, they won't be tearing it to
pieces to free you, but to strip you of those secret desires that dared
live outside the law. Enough of these little games, your sex doesn't
belong to you, give it back, it belongs to the Universal Order, to
Medicine, to the Family.

This libidinal dismembering will have what it takes to fluster
children, in fact. But if our doctors cheerfully doll up their characters with shame and uneasiness, it's only because such attitudes "are
useful in the psycho-affective maturation of the individual." And
the "counterbalance" of this "repressive system" (which, doubtlessly,
the poor little things have manufactured for themselves all alone, in
order to "develop freely" at a distance from horrible things having
to do with sex) will consist in rehabilitating… shame itself, by
turning it into the essential and attractive sentiment that makes
children cute like "tomatoes from the market."

From the market: they don't know how right they are. The purpose of the repressions, the goal of anti-sexual instruction, is not a
simple castration, an impediment to knowledge and pleasure: it's also
the re-education of the child's desire, so that it will show a servile
respect for the market codes of adult sexuality, including its hierar-
chies and taboos. This panicked conformity will be the sign that the
"individual" has attained his famous "psycho-affective maturity."

This is the second point that I'd like to make: the libidinal misappropriation of children by the family. The family doesn't totally "cut off" the sexuality of its "members"; it harnesses it, orients it, makes use of it through all the mitigations, all the perversions, all the masks. It's not through "authentic schoolwork" or in "camaraderie" that the child reinvests his inhibited desire: it's in family relations—with, as ancillaries, a few residual, solitary, ephemeral or shameful eroticisms. The outside world—friends, school—is useful to him only as a means of trying out, within little clans that copy public order, laws of the corporeal and libidinal market, whose main instruction and practice occur among one's own and behind locked doors.

Libidinal family-centralization, of which the work I am discussing gives some too perfect but revealing examples, is composed of two stages. First, the child as sexed subject is discredited; in the economy of the family he becomes a neuter object, nondesiring but desirable and able to be gratified with pleasures—a way of recognizing that his desire exists and that all of it must be made use of by keeping it unnamed and buried. The doctors in the *Encyclopedia* even want that elimination to be so total that the child doubts having had sex organs when he was little: after the description of these organs, Jean thinks about it, then exclaims, "We had all that when we were born?" Yes, but it was hidden from all of you because you were criminals—and to prove it, Dad tells the story of Oedipus:

"There's a period in childhood, around the age of three, when little girls become more attached to their father, and little boys to their mother. The child begins to notice the difference between the sexes of his parents, and also begins to notice their harmony, their intimacy. He doesn't like sleeping alone, whereas the two of them sleep in the same bed... The little boy becomes instinctively jealous of his father. He gets the impression that his father is stealing his mom from him at night!"

"Did we do that?" say the children, astounded.

What a useful discovery! In the few lines of a story, you've shown that a child's desire is bad—"instinctively" incestuous, selfish and cruel; that heterosexuality, conjugality, the need for sexual ownership over others are spontaneous and universal; that sons' hate for their fathers is a pathetic amorous jealousy, that a balanced older boy shouldn't feel it, because it would prove that he's still a baby, that he's sick; that "Mom," wife and mother, is the center of the world; that the solitary confinement of children under the authority of their parents and the erotic bell jar created by it, with its inequalities and prohibitions, is a natural and unavoidable stage in the destiny of every human.

The wonder is that the oedipal situation no longer seems anything but a string of crimes that the little child wanted to commit, and not the consequence of the conflict of impulses inflicted upon him by this parents. But in recounting the tale of Oedipus as if it were an "instinctive" and inevitable phenomenon, we legitimize that small socio-cultural horror known as the modern Western family—a kind of psychosexual cannibalism among three or four starving people tarred with the same brush. And we teach that desire has its original sin, and that therefore it must be corrected, controlled, directed, redeemed in order for it to become good. *Did we do that?* Afraid so, every human is born guilty, dreams only of murder and incest: if we hadn't forbidden you certain things, take a little look at where you would have been, you poor little wretches!

I'm not concerned with critiquing the oedipal pattern itself, the way in which psychoanalysis constructed it and the way it has been pulled totally to pieces since then: what interests me is the role that this pattern has been made to play when it is recounted to children—and this role is hateful. It reminds us that sexology is only interested in Freudianism to borrow from it new tools of family-centric indoctrination and the repression of desire.

Therefore, if the child forgets, conveniently conceals his sex and plays the oedipal game wholeheartedly, he'll be rewarded with affection, respect, flattery from Dad-Mom; he'll be fed, protected, hugged, rarely beaten; but if not, there will be persecution, pain, war. This is the second stage of libidinal misappropriation: you'll love us enough to desire and beg for what we'll give you—but you won't desire us too much, and, above all, you won't desire any other person on the outside. This is a deal for survival: the child who doesn't subscribe to it risks his hide. Unfortunately, I'm not referring to a metaphor: refusing the oedipal bargain means nothing less than attracting bad treatment that goes so far as murder. The infanticide committed by parents—on those of their offspring of "oedipal" age—has today actually become one of the very first causes of infant mortality. At the end of this chapter, I'll return to this monstrous aspect of family reality, whose importance few have had the daring to reveal to us—especially in France, where parental power and its crimes are better protected than anywhere else.

Last stage of the libidinal harnessing of children: any occasion for extrafamilial pleasure (being seduced by friends, by images, by writings, by adult strangers) will be denounced, forbidden, morally stigmatized, prevented by laws and in reality almost impossible; it will be the capital offence, and the child knows that there is no excuse and no pity for it. No sex outside, no sex inside: work-family for the child, while the barracks teaches his big brothers the meaning of the homeland.

The family in the *Encyclopedia* play at being nudists; so the little boy walks around with his prick exposed to the air, if not up in the air. But Mom, in the mode of right-thinking Freudian, describes the detrimental consequences of certain "regressions" to which children poorly integrated into the family would be prey:

...All of you are sure about our affection! [But when a] child feels abandoned, he continues to live like a baby, know what I mean? He's capable of doing anything to get attention... Even opening his fly in public!

Thus, there's a situation when a child is allowed to show his cock, it's good, it's a proof of mental health; and another situation when it's so bad that the guilty party must be immediately dragged to a psychotherapist, that courageous policeman of flies in revolt. Family nudity is innocent, it isn't done to "get attention"; however, in public nudity is perverse because it's showing something. The penis shown according to dad-mom's orders is a cut-off, missing pee-pee, whose very presence demonstrates its inexistence; the penis shown according to the child's initiative is a cock, a real one, autonomous, aggressive, desiring.

By what roundabout means, actually, does a child, "deprived of affection," open his fly in public? Is it really by means of it that you obtain another's affection? That would be too choice, in fact. Marriage agencies would close up shop, and the advice columns would change their tune.

I see two levels of explanation for this kind of child's behavior. You can show your prick either to suppress it, or to make it exist. Considering the sexual system for children, it's probably that the majority of those who show their cock, far from being unbalanced, abandoned or unfortunate, do it from a naïve hope, from pride and from desire: my dad, my mom, my brother, my sister don't want my cock, what about you?—that is all that is meant by this fine gesture, and it's a proof of great health, because it expresses the fact that such children aren't guilty enough to refrain, nor oedipal enough to make do with the very platonic family-style of fondling. But these kids scandalize; and their frank and innocent way of acknowledging that they desire to be desiring and desired will be called pathological.

In the same way, until the age of seven or eight, little children spontaneously express, with sensuality and an extreme eroticism, their liking for others; and it's not that they are begging to be mothered by every Tom, Dick and Mary; it's that their desire, immediately, crudely, invests itself in every affection that an older person's inspires in them—and that they secretly hope that the sources of pleasure that are called neither mom nor dad won't oppose their body with the oedipal flat refusal, which, through the prohibition of incest, teaches prohibition, plain and simple.

But since the *Encyclopedia* has denied the sexuality of the child, it refuses to interpret the display of it in terms of desire, autonomy, freedom. All it has left as explanation is a paltry pattern of regression. However, this will reveal the system of sexual alienation and the family-centric deal with which the child's desire is struggling.

We have followed, on one hand, the description of a boy spoiled by parental affection, but who castrates himself for the right to it; and on the other hand, a boy "neglected" because his parents don't love him and no one else has the right to love him. If he shows his cock in public, it's for it to be cut off like all children's and for him to receive, in compensation, his share of affection.

Little Jean, whose cock has been sacrificed to his family in exchange for tenderness, obeys that very law; and his innocence, his dreadful preadolescence, is actually a sign of the mutilating adaptation of his pleasures to the very specific erotic-castrator context that his parents are imposing upon him. That his penis is a detached, foreign object for him goes without saying, because that's its only currency of exchange: give your prick (he has learned), you'll get a sweet, a kiss, a day without trauma, one less spanking, some good sentiments, you'll be fondled, your nice mom will hug her "big sulky boy" again.

In conformity with the logic of this deal, a kid who is feeling helpless will offer his excrements or his pee-pee, one way or another, to pay for the affective benefit that his family circle is refusing him. The little exhibitionist, who moves our mater-analyst to pity, is like a brat who has peed in bed: he reproduces an outmoded organic market deal, a giving-to-get that's the first relationship to others that his parents have inculcated in him. He "continues to live like a baby," in fact: but no more nor less than Jean, the boy who has adjusted, who is doing the same actions, making the same demand—only Jean has family partners who respect the laws that they've established. The child exhibitionist, on the other hand, is in a desert; he "plays" his part in the castration, but there is no one opposite him to take the complementary role; and he fails, becomes a delinquent, whereas the others, who succeed, are good, well-behaved children.

The truth is, in its specifically family-centric and oedipal quality, that deal is only for private use; for the purpose of theater, it requires a "harmonious" family, where the adults have the time, strength and inclination to gratify the child a lot. Among those nice middle class people educated by *Elle*, if not by *Lui*, the wife is emancipated and the husband is big brother; motherhood is peacefully incestuous, or even like being the madam of a brothel (you produce handsome, well-dressed, well-fed, well-washed children, who are photographed, shown on television, and who arouse everybody, but nobody can fondle them but mom, who, in short, plays cockteaser with her kids in between); and fatherhood is slyly pedophilic. As long as the sex organ is always absent. Always indicated, however, by the care with which serious parents and docile children take to avoid it, so that it's a matter of conversations, sights or physical contact between big and small:

"*Since Sylvie was very little,*" says Jean, "*you've always given in to her funny faces! 'Give me a cuddle, Dad,'*" added the little boy, aping his sister.

"*I give in to your funny faces, too, my little wild man! Only with you, cuddles are more like fights... Obviously, between men...*" answers Dad.

What a fine example of a "polymorphously perverse" little boy put back on the straight and narrow by a father conscious of his duties. Pederasty satisfied and avoided at the same time by this pugnacious "cuddle" becomes for Dad, we see, a new way to teach his son the role-of-the-father. I sense with what excitement the authors, who "know," among other things, that their young readers "are" slightly homosexual, have set up that pedophiliac scene to convince them that, in this case as well, the family will be involved, and that it's useless to turn to one's friends, to adult strangers: no matter how complaisant they are about "little wild ones'" "funny faces," they wouldn't teach either the role of the father, or that of the son—nor even that of the daughter, whatever they may say. You've got to avoid them. Besides, Dad has a lot more advantages: he's right there, he's tall, handsome, he has money, he's got two babes under his heel and he lets you grope them a little, in fact he has the good taste to "allow" you to have it all while reminding you that "between men" you hit 'em, "obviously," right on the kisser, just as fond Nature would have it, but that there are women there for the peace and quiet of these noble warriors. Women, really? For Jean and his funny faces? Uh, not right away: you have to earn the hole. Dad points at it like preachers indicate Paradise: it's always beyond, and it's by obeying that you buy the right to enter it. Not me or that, murmurs Dad with—all the same—a tender indulgence for the muddled and touching appetites of his little look-alike.

Look-alike? Not in age or body, but only by blood and sex—which is already too much, since, in order for two to taste pleasure, they have to be "complementary." What does it mean to be "complementary"? Clearly, nobody knows a thing about it; it comes down to a nasty little calculation of similarities and differences. A screw "is" complementary to a nut, but a dog "isn't" complementary to a cat, despite the fact that both of them have fur, teeth, ears that stick up and a tail that moves; *only, their cuddles are like fights*, since they're of different breeds. However, there are a number of perverted dogs that run after cats, not to bite them but to sniff their hole and lick their muzzles affectionately. A cat's soft, it smells good, it's small, it goes fast, you marvel that it exists; cats marvel, too, they're stunned that some goof with big paws and too long a nose is running his nostrils over their body. Perhaps "complementarity" is such an affinity, which isn't concerned with race, age, sex or money. But all intercourse that ignores sex, age, race, money is damned by our society. Doctors, who aren't the latest to add their yapping to the imprecations currently in usage, have in this way defined the only kind of complementarity that the sexual order can allow: the one that produces children. It begins with sexes that are biologically complementary: but after that, how can a solid couple, a balanced home, a happy family be established if the parents aren't of the same race, the same social roots, and don't belong to the same generation? One exclusion leads to another, and from antihomosexuality to racism and age segregation, the step is so easy that doctors won't take it themselves: it's up to the reader to understand, for example from his neighbors, how to construct an orthodox type of happiness. This is how biological complementarity and social complementarity are confused; the second adds its own shackles, discriminations, arbitrariness, infamies to the first, and all that becomes "natural" is what respects the ethnic, sexual and social prejudices of the good, well-intentioned people around you who've discovered those great truths during their latest soap opera or their last red wine.

The ideology of the complementarity of the sexes is by definition nonegalitarian, mercantile, characteristic of a society of exploitation. It demands that we base a number of cultural differences on the morphological and functional differences between men and women (and between children and adults); without this compartmentalization and these ploys, "good" sexuality collapses. The *Encyclopedia*, which wants to be democratic and sensitive to the demands of women, therefore attempts to teach sexual equality while at the same time preserving the established differences needed by its reactionary conception of the sexual order. During the entire dialogue, they pretend that Jean thinks of himself as superior to Sylvie and that his parents are demonstrating to him that he's wrong—*what a new idea* (barely two centuries old, in fact)—and the pathetic text, which is as deft as a nice lady fighting racism by claiming that negroes aren't all vicious, that Arabs wash as much as we, that there are generous Jews and virile queers, accumulates blunder after blunder:

Corporal equality:

"Seen from the back, you look a lot alike! (says Mom to Jean and Sylvie).

Sexual equality:

Sylvie sighs, "And all I have is a slit! No penis, no testi—...um, like you said..."

"But yes, my darling, you have sex organs, too. Hidden inside your plump little tummy!... You'll never have a penis, just a canal, the vagina."

"Oh, I've got a vagina!" says Sylvie, very happy with herself..."

Mental equality:

"So my little girl has the gift of logic?" notes Dad with pleasure. "You're right, my little blue kitten."

Equality in the face of puberty:

Jean: *"I'll have a beard and a moustache!"*

"After that, I'll be a man!"

"You'll be as proud as a peacock..."

"You are already... You're producing a little bit of male hormone."

Sylvie: *puts on her most miserable look and murmurs, "I'm a girl, not a woman..." Mom consoles her: "Puberty comes earlier for girls... you'll become a woman..."*

"Will I have a bust?"

"Your breasts will start growing at around twelve, darling, I promise you!" Jean swiftly retorts, "Be careful! Dad said that it was a weird period of time..."

"...Sometimes, during it, little girls are not as pretty," says Dad gently. "Their skin gets oilier, they often get pimples, blackheads..."

"Oh, great," moans Sylvie, discouraged.

Social equality for little girls:

"I'm going to high school, too, next year! And I'll take courses!" explodes Sylvie. "And I'll even be an engineer like Dad!"

Social equality for women:

"You see (says Dad), *Mom succeeded at doing something very difficult but yet indispensable... She knew how to keep her femininity intact while working at a man's job. She works as much as I do, but"*—adds Dad with tenderness—*"she preserves a privileged place for love and pleasure."*

This compendium truly discourages all commentary. I'd prefer to first paraphrase and invert a few passages, to do better justice to their idiocy:

"Jean sighs: 'And I have no slit! No vulva, no clito—… um, like you said…'"

"But you do, my little red chicken, you have sex organs, too, hanging from the outside of your plump little tummy!… You'll never have a vagina, only a tube, the penis."

"'Oh, all I've got is a penis,' says Jean, full of shame. He put on his most miserable look: 'I'm a little boy, not a woman…' Mom consoles him: 'Puberty comes later for boys… You won't be as pretty, you'll have pimples, blackheads.'

"I won't have a bust?"

"Your testicles are going to get bigger, but I can't promise you. Still, you'll have a beard, a moustache."

"Oh, great!" moans Jean, discouraged.

"You see," says Mom, "Dad failed at something that was indispensable, and yet easy… He didn't know how to keep his virility intact, and he's working at a very idiotic job. Not only did he work less than me, but"—Mom adds angrily—"he didn't devote any place to love or pleasure."

Such a portrait of your average forty-year-old French person seems curiously close to reality to me; however, all I wanted to do above was write the opposite of what Dad expects from Mom. In inverting that eulogy for the ideal woman, I could have fabricated a negative male monster of the kind that exists nowhere: but I ended up with a family kind of father. The conclusion to draw from this is obvious enough.

And it's very clear as well that the finest principles of sexual equality are only hypocrisy and a lie, because of the extent to which we remain attached to the pro-birth obsession. The burden of procreation isn't the same for men as it is for women: from the moment a woman has to be a mother, that overwhelming biological servitude will continue to be exploited to the nth degree by the male and by the sexual order.

From then on, freedoms, the easing-up society allows women, won't do away with the old slavery; they will add to it, and the woman will have the right to work, vote, have an abortion, provided that she first fulfills her old roles: baby-maker, caretaker of the home, bottom-wiper, cook, slattern, maid for the children and Dad's whore.

"Can a woman live and work without having a child?"

"Of course, but that's a new idea," answers Dad, who moves on immediately to praising his own wife, his model wife, because she's a "mom" despite her "man's job," and because her professional responsibilities don't prevent her from allowing herself to get fucked by Dad and only by Dad and only when he wants to.

All women who work (and who don't belong to the well-to-do middle class of the *Encyclopedia*) know that this mixture of sexual submission, domestic servitude and salaried slavery is "difficult," and desperately live it every day.

But as for it being "indispensable," really, that's asking a bit much. A woman who is alone and childless has the right to exist, "of course"; nevertheless, in the sauce of motherhood and marriage in which we swim, she'll seem—and perhaps think she is—a woman deprived of all true happiness. As neither wife nor mother, she loses no chains; on the contrary, she has lost the most precious thing she had: her "femininity."

The little girl being indoctrinated will listen—since you must be objective—to a description of the self-sufficient woman: a creature who's hard-hearted, frosty, austere, undesired, too "modern." The childless woman isn't a woman, the childless couple is living a great tragedy, the single mother, in fact, doesn't exist. What's left? The "real" woman, beautiful, fulfilled, bursting with happiness, showered with praise—the one who arouses men's "affection," the respect of patriots and the interest of employers: the married mom who works.

The entire *Encyclopedia* is devoted to that ploy: yes, it says, you "can" be free sexually; but if you want to be happy, balanced, well accepted by others, it's better to give up on it. You love gilt, garlands? Only cages have them around here—whereas freedom is only grief, frustration, loneliness. That's how things are: up to you to "choose."

The lot of the mother, as opposed to that ticket to religion, the single person, will appear to be female happiness par excellence, because the only way that the body, sex, growth, amorous pleasures, the social future of girls is presented is as a function of motherhood. And in order to demonstrate this more clearly to little girls, the authors have no qualms about rectifying women's anatomy. Delighted at having "just a vagina," Sylvie would probably be even "happier" to have a clitoris: but as incredible as it may seem, our doctors haven't deigned to tell her.

The vagina is academic intercourse, a husband, procreation; the clitoris, as everyone knows, is about jerking off, orgasm without the male and without a cock, lesbianism—in short, what allows you to come without being either lover, spouse or mother. That's why it's excised in many paternalist societies; invariably the sexologists, whose only standard is "nature," but who retouch it without scruples as soon as it disturbs the sexual order, inveigh against the clitoris and expel it to its niche as a small satellite of great vaginal pleasure. Sexual "information" for preadolescents must not name an appendage that is so suspect and so dangerous.

For the same reason, the book has disregarded the female orgasm, and we saw that earlier. Dad is lying on Mom, he "ejaculates," and that's "orgasm." Certainly this must be an egalitarian protocol, because the husband and wife have "found" the movement of coitus "together"... But, just as all other situations and all other means of female pleasure are censored, young female readers will come to the conclusion that for a woman, having an orgasm is merely helping yourself to a bit of male pleasure—waiting for a man, a husband, to climb on top of you and "instinctively" do what's described in the book. It's that or nothing.

And even though clitoral masturbation plays an enormous role in French conjugal life (Dad sticks it to her and then goes to sleep, Mom jerks off after), we pass over it in silence. This doesn't keep it from existing, but for mothers and daughters masturbation will remain disgraceful, shameful, squalid and not nice. That's all that counts in the eyes of "science."

In compensation, there will be long, poetic descriptions of pregnancy and its physical pleasures. Mom sighs:

"I remember a symphony by Mozart. It was four or five months before Jean was born. I was at the concert with Dad, and Jean moved inside me for the first time... I told Dad, who squeezed my hand hard, very hard. He looked at me, very moved... We'd become "three," and I'll never be able to forget that feeling of total fulfillment."

There's not a bodice button left unpopped in this scene of refined emotion, this unique moment in love, this panegyric in a tone of middle class good taste; a pulp romance writer couldn't do any better. Little girls will wet their drawers. Becoming with foal—this is the "fulfillment" of women who are loved, this fine tale informs them. It's more like a cow's happiness—whom, apparently, we also make listen to Mozart in the barn so that it will have more milk. Modern agriculture is blessed with such refinements.

Juliette, it must be remembered, "wants" the baby she's carrying; this desire even makes her "blush." The relationship between the mother and the fetus is in fact only admitted with propriety; she is in love.

"My baby keeps awfully quiet... That night, on the other hand, I was entitled to a few heel kicks..."

"He'll play rugby!" declares Jean, riotously happy.

"I stroked my stomach, to show him a sign of friendship."

Invariably, the baby is a boy: once more, "complementarity" is the gauge for success—all the more because pregnancy will be less attractive if you have to impose it on yourself only to reap the second-rate human product known as a girl. And Sylvie marvels at the fact that you can have such a well-lodged lover all to yourself:

With infinite gentleness the little girl places her hand on Juliette's "big belly": "He moved!" she says.

"He's getting rowdy... He needs a bit more space, he's chosen a position that he'll hardly change until birth."

"With his head in back, or sitting on his little bottom?"

A strange perversion instilled in little girls, this desire to have a little boy moving in their bellies. ("Do you have to move?" Jean was asking in relation to coitus.) Meanwhile, any fears that could be inspired by delivery will be dismissed:

"And aren't you just a tiny bit afraid?" says Sylvie, surprised.

"Why would I be afraid?" answers Juliette. "I know everything that will happen, and I won't be alone. My husband will be with me."

Once more, husband-love-baby form but one affective knot that is the desirable itself. *Boy or girl, what's the difference?* Sylvie was saying: and she was demanding to be an engineer "like Dad." Too bad that the book, in fact, only teaches her to be pregnant like Mom.

Before I was pointing out that in this work meant for children older than 10 and younger than 14, the boys were represented by a kid of 11, who is prepubescent and mentally backward. But for the girls, the authors have dared even more: their heroine, with all of her 9 years, isn't even old enough to read the manual in which she appears.

Such brazen infantilizing allows them, quite probably, to neglect the questions that a 12- or 13-year-old heroine would have asked. These young readers' presence is only Sylvie's future; the adolescence they're experiencing is only a "discouraging" but far-away nightmare for our little girl. And what's more, it was very convenient for the girl to be her brother's younger sibling and not the older one: in this way, the hierarchy of the sexes is respected and, in fact, even decency; as for "equality," it will be taught as a duty of compassion, a kindness that the boys, because of their superiority, will impose upon themselves in their behavior toward the girls—those disabled idiots who will enjoy male freedom on the sole condition that none of their privileges are changed.

Jean is "already a man"; as for Sylvie, she's neither man, woman, boy (except "from the back"), nor girl: she's a blue kitten with a clitorectomy, who splashes around in her rustic ingenuousness, and whose *most cherished dream* is to have "a bust" so she can place a brat on it.

Women and girls, who are omnipresent in the form of uteruses, stand aside in a very small corner of the picture as soon as it's a question of pleasure. Even the kind for prisoners: masturbation. The subject is broached by a dialogue between father and son; Mom shuts up; *Sylvie listens to the conversation absent-mindedly*—she herself has no "sex organs" to "touch," so...

Though a fraction of the French middle class, in their acceptance of certain "liberal" principals, tolerate the fact that their children jerk off, the prohibition against pleasure-for-one remains, as we know, very much in force; experienced by all those whom a more overly repressive generation has educated, masturbation is kept in a zone of silence and guilt. Nevertheless, the old excuses for forbidding masturbation are obsolete, and if they do survive, no one advertises it, apart from those in a parochial milieu. The avant-gardists of repression come close to opposing such Catholic hypocrisy: a truce for the witch hunt, they say, we've got more dangerous enemies. But they let the religious zealots devote themselves to their repressive little rubbish, the way you resign yourself to the fact that an old man who has regressed into childhood spills his soup, smells of urine and plays with his pooh. We liked the Christian order so much that we can easily pardon it its senility, and then, after all, that piece of furniture still comes in handy a bit at times, it distracts the adversary.

As for the *Encyclopedia* doctors, their indirect condemnation of masturbation certainly is the most perverted, the most obnoxious that I was able to read:

"Dad, the other day I saw a big guy from eighth grade who was writing on the door of a locker: Hurray for pleasure for one. *It made some other guys in my class laugh, but I didn't understand. Is there a pleasure for one?"*

"Yes, it's called masturbation. That 'big guy from eighth grade' was discovering the pleasure gotten from his own body, without a partner. That's why it's "for one."

"And you do it all alone?"

"You touch your sex organs. In high school you've probably heard the expression 'jerk off,' haven't you? (but I prefer using the accurate term, masturbation)."

"Ah, yes!"

"Well, that's the way you have pleasure for one. And I think that the graffiti by the big guy from eighth grade is only a sign that this boy is unhappy and can't talk to his father about the problems he's having with puberty… When parents refuse to provide their children with information… the troubled child becomes anxious, he feels abandoned. Losing interest in work, he withdraws more and more. He'll end up, for example, writing on the door of his locker, merely to protest his sexual destitution!"

"Is masturbation not allowed because it's dangerous?"

"No, masturbation isn't wrong or dangerous. But if a child gets to like it, it will be harder later to love someone else… And pleasure is better when it's shared. It's doubled, you know what I mean?"

Sylvie (who *"listened absent-mindedly"*) *concludes logically: "Jean, no writing on doors for you! All you have to do is reread the book with Dad…"*

Don't worry, little policewoman: Jean will never write on doors, nor walls, nor protest posters. This is a *fully developed high school student*, he'll be a hardworking schoolboy, a manageable conscript; he won't "protest" his "sexual destitution"—nor anything else, either.

Actually, what is a "sexual destitution," and how do you cure it? By masturbating? No. By having sex with a girl? No. With a boy? No. With a goldfish, a double amputee, a pair of ankle boots, an enema tube, a corpse, a piece of calf's liver? No. With Mom? No. With Dad? Aw, come on…

No. You take care of it by avoiding three dangers designated by the book, and thus imposing upon yourself the three severe rules that follow:

"don't 'isolate' yourself;

"have a 'taste for work'…;

"talk with your father about the 'problems brought on by puberty.'"

How novel: when temptation seizes you, you don't pray any more, and the book you run to to save your soul is no longer a missal, either; it's the *Hachette Encyclopedia*. Aside from that, the formula is still the same—the nudist father replaces the priest in his cassock, that's all.

What's Dad going to say, since any positive solution to "sexual destitution" has been prohibited? But of course he'll say the most positive thing in the world: stay near us, work and wait. Let's reread the book together. Look at the father, mother, baby. It'll all be yours some day. Doesn't that make it worth suffering a bit? Yes, Father, I'm ashamed of myself, I will think of Saint Family and I won't do it any more. I don't want to ruin my chances of being a Father "later on." Excellent, my son. Besides, when you're 14, I'm going to let you masturbate—the accurate term. *Moderately: 2 times a week at 14, 3 to 4 times a week at 16*, according to the magazine *Parents*, 1971. And you wonder: how do the parents in question manage to assure these healthy rates; does it have to be done in front of them? By what kind of spying on bedrooms or dirty linens do they become *aware of the fact that their child is incurring the habit of devoting himself immoderately to practices of such a nature*, which will prompt them, *Parents* continues, to *notify the doctor or psychologist who alone will know how to design the appropriate treatment.*

O.K., a treatment: since jerking off is "neither a vice nor a danger," but is prohibited even so, it certainly had to be a disease. Can you catch it from toilet seats?

Seems that you can, if you stay on one too long. All of a sudden, an icy dizziness seizes you, with horror you notice your own fingers "touching" your own "sexual organs," and—boom!—you're sick.

Detailed and precise as it is when it's a matter of orgasms leading to breeding or of the positions of a foetus, the text remains quite vague when it comes to this strange childhood disease. Let's reread the father's explanations and try to put them together into a coherent whole.

A boy, it says, discovers this solitary pleasure because his parents refuse to inform him (about the subject of conjugal pleasures?). He feels abandoned, so he isolates himself. Hmm. Strange remedy for abandonment. Once he's alone and upset, he touches his own body, a bizarre, paradoxical action that people with healthy minds don't do. But it's because nobody loves him, and this isn't very smart, because it will keep him from loving others later on. In other words, he's touching himself because he's alone, and he'll remain alone because he's touched himself.

Likewise, in summing up the arguments that "define" masturbation, we discover in condensed form a remarkable assertion: *pleasure for one is obtained by means of the expression* to jerk off, *an inaccurate term.*

That's what feels good, inaccurate terms? And what is it, exactly, touching? What do you touch? The "penis"? The "testi— *ahem?*" With your thumb? Your index finger? The cat's tail? A pair of tweezers? Like when you wash yourself, pulling down that little *fold of skin, the foreskin?* Holding all of it in your hand? which one? Do you do it roughly? gently? for how long? Is it "enough" to touch it with the end of your finger and then take it away very very fast, like when you touch a candle flame? It stings? Is "the penis" having an "erection"? Even when you're not sleeping? "Do you have to move" your hand? Do you "discover the movement"? Do you have to "have sperm," or does it work without it? So, is "sexual pleasure" possible before puberty? Why didn't you say so, Dad? Do girls also "touch" themselves? How do they do it, if all they have is "just a vagina"? Is it "orgasm," like when Dad makes a baby with Mom? Are you sitting down? Standing? On all fours? Hopping? With your legs in the air? Is it okay to watch? Can you sniff it? Can you put a finger in your butt? Two? Should you hide? In "a locker room"? And what if I touch myself in front of someone, is that still "for one"? It's not "shared"? You're sure? But if I touch him and he touches me this time, isn't it sharing? Why do you say no? It's no longer "sharing" as soon as you put your fingers there? So, you need a knife and fork, like at the table, when you "feel like some pastry"? Do you keep your hands behind your back when you make love? Where are you allowed to put them? Do you smack Mom in the face if she "touches" your "sex organs" before your "penis slips inside instinctively"? Is that why people get divorced? And why does "pleasure for one" make "the other guys in my class" laugh? Then, is it fun to be "unhappy"? Since our friends touch themselves, why haven't we ever tried, whereas we're free and not "ashamed of our bodies"? Why is it we never know anything any more when Dad explains things but know a bunch of things when Dad explains nothing? What about you Dad, do you jerk off?[9]

Explain the math to me, too, Dad. Why is pleasure "doubled" when it's "shared"?

---

9. According to the *Simon report*, 73% of French men (93% of Americans, according to the *Kinsey report*) do. On the other hand, only 19% of French women were familiar with masturbation (62% for Americans). Generally, this very low figure has been attributed to the extreme guilt women feel about the matter—but no one wants to say whether they're ashamed to the point of not jerking off, or if they do jerk off but refuse to "admit it," even for an anonymous survey. Note that when it comes to this subject, 14% of the men and 17% of the women in France explicitly refused to answer this question about their "pleasures for one"; and that, along with homosexuality, the subject seems to represent the most guilt-ridden aspect of French sexuality.

If I cut an apple in two, two of us can eat it, but each of us only gets half. What's more fun, eating an apple all by yourself or half an apple with somebody? It depends on whether you really like apples or that other person, right? But if I want to double the pleasure, I need two apples, not one. So if I jerk off twice, won't that double it?

And let's say: today I have an apple, and I give all of it to somebody; but tomorrow I have another apple, and I eat it all by myself. Is that bad? Do you really have to cut up pleasure for it to exist? But if it's doubled when there's two, it must be tripled when there's three, quadrupled when there's four, centupled when there's a hundred of you, right? Can a hundred people do it together? And if I get used to sampling it all alone, why is it that I won't love anybody else any more? Is it that good all by yourself and that bad with others?

It's clear how the prohibition against masturbation is reinstated: jerking off is neither physically dangerous nor perverted, you can't catch tuberculosis or, as family medicine has confirmed for less than a century, Pott's Disease. But this is a thousand times worse: you become unfit for love, unhappy, lonely, a deviant—a pariah. In short, jerking off is a psychological sin followed by social damnation.

Thus, in the discourse of the educator, we have a prohibition that no longer functions by the threat of direct punishment but by a kind of blackmail using "happiness."

Such a metaphysics copies that of the Church, and serves the same purpose. In the past, you lived your "earthly" life in preparation for your Salvation in the next: you had to suffer temporarily in order to be eternally happy. Brought down to earth, that system hasn't changed: the human being has some years of apprenticeship (family/school) that redeem him from his original sins (bestiality, ignorance, pointlessness, perversity, oedipal behavior) and prepare him for the beyond: adult happiness (production, ownership, power). And depending on what you've done during childhood, you'll go to paradise or to hell, once you grow up.

There is therefore nothing new about what I call blackmail using happiness: it's the stakes that have been brought nearer and that have been incarnated here down below. Indoctrination merely works better. The writers of the past denounced the "impiety" of their contemporaries, whom the prospect of eternal happiness wasn't enough for remaining resigned to the suffering inflicted by the class in power. Now that the happiness isn't consumed beyond the clouds any more, these moralists have nothing left to criticize: because by the most complete submission, each of us strives to obtain these visible, factory-made pleasures that come from familiar sources. It's just a matter of social conformism, rewarded day after day; and the only hell becomes being different—not belonging to the privileged bourgeoisie, or at least to its workforce.

All those who blemish the smooth, clean image of capitalist prosperity are put on the sidelines, far from our streets, public places, daily life, contact with others; countless official or secret prisons hide the millions and millions of men and women who don't match the proper model—underpaid workers, whether French or immigrant, indigent old people, orphans, the physically ugly, the "handicapped," the infirmed, law-breakers, "deviants," those "with a screw loose," dissenters, loners, simpletons. And now we know what the Elect we were told about in the catechism look like, those to whom paradise-society opens its gates: the *Encyclopedia* has 90 pages of photos. The young-but-not-too-insipid-looking senior executive in perfect health, with his orthodox values, a model consumer and high-tech producer with a hyperregulated brain; he and his livestock represent both what you have to be to deserve happiness and what kind of happiness you get. (No need to point out the similarity between these images and those used in ads for ordinary or luxury products: advertising's "modern man" has only one face, whether it's to sell pro-birth values or razor blades, the government in power or cheese "slowly and naturally ripened in cellars.")

And in a society where all people talk about are defiance, challenge, revolution, never has the respect for social codes been so great, adherence to the system more unconscious or avid, never have we had to do so much to receive so little. Vigilant spying on one another; the deprecation and expulsion that results from the slightest deviance from class stereotypes, from the clan, the family; that unbelievable mixture of aggression, greed and denial that define our relations with others; our "private life," conceived as a state of blissful retreat in comparison to our unbearable "social life" (institutions, work, living under the same roof with someone): all of it adds up to a host of pressures that are so overwhelming and so irrefutable that it's redundant to preach that human beings should submit to them; they know very well what happens when they're careless enough to deviate from them, no matter how slightly.

Because deviance signifies a lot more than difference: it means that you're placing yourself in the hands of the other, the hands of power; that you're ceasing to be an independent—i.e., redeemed—individual and that everyone will have the right to cast the first stone; that you're becoming a "special case"—a discredited member of society.

Too long a nose, too short in height, a slightly flat chest, an idea that's a bit new immediately put your right to exist in danger. And among our people, prosperity, a great upsurge in racism and segregation are the most visible aspects of a mania for discrimination found everywhere, about everything, all the time, a paranoid mechanism that degrades our perception of others and of ourselves.

Beyond what is politely called the social classes, our society tends to fragment into an infinite number of "minorities," families, formed officially or not by those whose particular peculiarity differentiates them from the accepted model—they're everywhere. From "Handicapped Family Names" (for people who think they have a ridiculous last name) to the homosexual, the range of the "abnormal" is limitless, because everything that refers to a human being, everything that makes him visible is now a reason for persecution— or creates the feeling that you're inferior to others and therefore ill adapted for the path to happiness. In addition, normality is sold to those who can pay for it; it will increase their value on the sexual, professional and cultural—not to mention, ethnic—market. Among plastic surgery for the nose, boobs or butts; the rectification of brains and morals; enculturation by mail; huge sales of uniformity of every feather (clothes, furniture, food, newspapers); even the array of dyed-in-the-wool antiestablishment stuff that allows you to pass unnoticed (noticed/valorized) in student neighborhoods (the book you must have under your arm, the American- style thrift-store junk you must have on your ass), we see the same business frenetically distributing signs of belonging, transmitting order, self-effacement, orthodoxies—accesses to happiness.

I'm recalling these obvious things to point out that propaganda based on blackmail using happiness, far from being an easing of an old, repressive system, is resorting to real forces and sources of authority that currently regulate coexistence among human beings. Hand in hand with this theoretical order, these laws and this explicit ideology is that empirical and voracious order that all children and adults, rebels and reactionaries, poor and rich, clever and imbecilic understand, respect, reproduce without being asked to and reinforce without being forced to. At a last degree of strangulation, faced with the impossibility of existing and desiring, members of a moribund society are using the following tactic: they collect from the rubbish of a ruined order any shred of code, rules or prohibition available and fashion it into an instrument of savage power over others—then use that weapon pitilessly, until they've managed to save their own hides.

In the context of such a pleasant form of modernity, telling a child that committing such and such an act puts him at risk for becoming different from everyone else later on is actually threatening him with a death sentence. It hasn't taken him 10 or 12 years to learn that "difference" is the greatest crime: groups of children punish and exclude their members—him, too—for the slightest peculiarity, the least breach of code, and insist upon their authoritarian hierarchy of pleasures, values, powers. These interactions, modeled on those of the Order of the family, are an essential doublet of it; and you could certainly claim that recreation teaches the child more about normality than hours in the classroom could ever inflict upon him. The reproduction of order within a group of children is an intense experience; obedience is the primary aspect of a market in which the child trades in his useless freedom for group acceptance, which converts all sources of pleasure into capital. Submission, torments, sacrifices, as long as there is escape from isolation, from its physical and emotional desolation. The child who is banished by others (or the one who banishes himself from them) is condemned (or condemns himself) to a loathsome daily frustration, and also becomes the preferred victim of the group. A body with no owner, nationality or brand, he is like virgin territory waiting to be ravaged by the horde, lost cash that the group can snatch and squander: to be "saved," you have to "belong."

This dual status—an isolated body defined as different and unique and cut off from the sources of pleasure, but a body nevertheless, indeterminate, exposed to violence, subject to being comandeered yet remaining unmarketable—is what terrorizes children. Such a painful form of autonomy is useless, and the loneliness is worse than a state of simple insufficiency. Since children don't own their bodies, in a society where such private ownership is the only protection of the body, the only way for a child to save what is his is by fusing with group ownership, gang, family.

Wielding the threat of solitary confinement—or, loss—is precisely how the father in the text I have just quoted persuades his son not to masturbate. Once he becomes an adult, the child escapes the danger of being destroyed, squandered, as a result of the privatization of the body—which the pre-adolescent child will himself achieve, gradually and under certain conditions. But his father warns him that if he tries to enjoy his limited degree of ownership, he'll immediately lose its advantage and will find himself forever after confronted by dangers that it was supposed to ward off.

You think you're privatizing your body in the name of pleasure, whereas you're actually turning it into an object of exploitation, harnessed, molded and motivated in a way that the exploiting system can gain control of and put it in its place so that there is no spillage. As long as the child's body can't be economically exploited, the family holds on to it and inculcates it with privatization by the deprivation of pleasure: a nonprivate and nonproducing body is a weak and frustrated body, whereas a privatized and producing body equals autonomy and access to thrill. In this way, sexuality is defined for minors as a profit machine, reserved for adults: you place your body in it to put it in action, and it pays you a revenue—pleasure. The child's mind is cured of all temptation to act any other way; if he got the habit of using his body without investing it, he'd discover that pleasure is possible outside the deal, without submitting to the apparatus of exploitation—you can eat the bait without getting caught in the trap.

Sexuality in public and free forms of pleasure will become diseases, they'll lead to prison or being grouped with the insane. Placation of desire will have to be associated with an ideal state of withdrawal: in the language intended for age 7–9, "desiring" translates as *liking to be alone with someone*. You're a nudist, but behind the wall of family ownership—or inside a puritanical community cleansed of all desire, in which you take off your own clothes because a communal kind of clothing, enclosure, fence immediately reclothes you.

Making love as well means withdrawing to the most private part of a private place: night, bed, shut-up room. Parents recount the "matrimonial" act by showing virtuous scientific photos that are "informative" but hide what the slightest pornographic picture—though it's "obscene"—objectively reveals. The example of a conjugal kiss won't be taken from the home, the street, the subway, where children see it constantly (though they "shouldn't"): it will be chosen from a scene in a movie. This private ritual is only visible and decent to the extent that it's marketable—in other words, staged—and therefore vindicated of the offence of exhibitionism. Such a strange telescoping of the kiss combines the obligation of showing it with that of keeping it at a distance—upholding the distance between the child and "sexuality" and, within that sexuality, between the subject-role, which is public, and the pleasure-roles, withheld unless profit (a movie) justifies their deprivatization.

Such is the law of this situation, which bourgeois legalese vocabulary has transparently dubbed: a carnal transaction.

This book has described how the economic pattern must be constructed, with its distribution of profits: the man will be the owner of the family, whereas his wife, as usufructuary, will have the pleasure of the children produced by the couple. This transaction secures a return on desire and constitutes the profitable model of investment to which it must conform.

But the child must also accept the complex system assigned to him by this model. At first, he must serve as the reward-object for his parents; his body is both privatized and collective—collectivized because it belongs to all family members, and private because access is prohibited to strangers on the "outside." During the first years of his life, this contradictory obligation (you must privatize when you're "outside," collectivize when you're "inside"), complicated by a host of exceptions and code-breaking, and increased twofold by the oedipal sexual taboo (the familial collectivization of the child's body excludes the genital regions, or, should we say, takes an interest in them just to ban them) becomes for him a terrifying riddle—causing, in fact, quite a few riddled brains.

Later on, the child must gradually recover his body, his sex, and learn to reproduce the corresponding social role; without, however, such privatization, in which the sex remains unused ("frozen" capital), inciting him to sample any type of pleasure.

The duty to be sexual/not sexual is, obviously, unlivable; and the contradiction is resolved by oscillating from one pole to the other, from sex to non-sex according to circumstances, parents, friends, waves of self-repression—as well as the workings of the glands, which will soon lead to the protrusion of the genital zone beyond censorship, like the tip of an iceberg above the frozen ocean in which it remains engulfed. The "sex organs" become the only locus of sexuality, because in 12 or 13 years of living, you learn to prevent desire from dwelling just anyplace, sex included: but because of puberty, sex is what "pops up" even so. The rest of the body will remain forever shut up—if not for occasional leaks catalogued by the "pathology" of sexuality and that medicine persists in stitching up with foaming mouth and reddened eyes.

This moment of emergence and reappearance of sex on the "outside" of the armored body cordoned off by education is the thorn in the side of the flunkies and pigs who control the cattle of childhood. The danger is that this emergence isn't content with slightly transgressing the censorship of the body, which would only let by an incomprehensible pee-pee or keep within limits a vulva already rendered more or less frightening by the drama of first menstruation for girls kept in ignorance. No, enveloping repression certainly can be completely broken down, bringing to light an anus, hands, a mouth, skin, and revealing that the body and sex are no more than one: and this wastrel of a desiring body, undivided and integral, will gallop away without your suspecting it and without your being able to ever get it back.

Normally, if family repression is skillfully accomplished and if surveillance, monitoring, indoctrination are increased during this sensitive years, there's nothing very serious to worry about: there will be nothing but a slight itching in the area of the "organs." It's explained to the child that he mustn't scratch and that it will grow all by itself. Once it has popped out or is gaping, hairy, ready for use in the rituals of matrimony, it will be time to move on to the next repressive phase, the "difficult age."

At this point, the parents need only keep the child from exploiting the progressive privatization of his body within the family (sleeping alone, washing alone, studying alone, crossing the street alone, to some degree choosing his clothing, his leisure activities, his words, his objects, etc.: being less and less at the mercy of the eyes, gestures, touches, corporeal culture of his parents). All of a sudden the child is beginning to have "his own" body: capital to manage. The degree of autonomy of management allowed him by his family will depend, among other things, on how much they trust him: if he's managing his body as he has been taught, or if he knows how to pretend he is, everything will be fine. But if some weakness, emotion, fantasy, irregularity, disorder, "vice" shows that he can't or doesn't want to accept this privatization in an orthodox way, there will be a step backward, his body will be again taken in hand, or he'll be sent to a psychotherapist to be handled, or to boarding school, to a "reform" school. This is the period during which the results of twelve years of slavery are verified; and if the results are flawed, some rapid, brutal measures toward "recovery" are taken: for there is very little time left before the child must be freed and, willy-nilly, let out into the world of "commerce."

The entire book for ages 10–13 touches only upon two aspects of its readers' sexuality: masturbation, which must be prohibited (as a "premature" exploitation of privatization that risks causing deviancy); and seduction by strangers, which must also be prohibited (as "premature" sexual commerce, which risks not being commerce at all and becomes the child's crime of body management, which is endangered in regards to its marketable normalcy).

Let's take another look at the first point, before focusing on how the authors have dealt with the second. *If a child gets to like masturbation*, says Dad, *it will be harder later to love someone else.* This "harder" will be considered admirable: for Dad, it's understood, "to love someone else" is always difficult, but if you jerk off, it will be even "more difficult." The difficulty preoccupying Dad, of course, is fulfilling a good marriage contract. Loving *someone else* (would it be more "natural" to love oneself?) represents an impressive leap forward, the adventure of a petit-bourgeois with cane and hat wandering into the jungle and becoming fascinated by an extra-familial being, a passion that borders on eccentricity and extravagance—an idea that goes well with the ban on all sexual expenditure, which it serves to justify. Expending is dangerous. Looking, desiring, touching are dangerous. And solitary consumption, without looking at anybody, without "desiring," but nonetheless touching, is dangerous, too. No "pleasure for one," no squandering, nothing gratuitous: you could "get to like it," not jerking off, but pleasure-in-and-for-itself, by yourself, or with two, or a thousand. You'll deviate from the middle class economic schema of libidinal investment, and this is the schema to which it will become very hard to conform "later on."

A "good" child doesn't try to steal pleasure for himself. He conscientiously preserves himself until the very last day of his contract. Thus Jean has no knowledge of his sex, he doesn't even imagine that you could touch your prick: his is as faraway as the Moon, it's in Dad's hands. Nevertheless, the question he asks lets us know that he's a bit more informed than he lets on. In fact, he doesn't ask, "It's not allowed?" He says, "It's not allowed because it's dangerous?"

Dad isn't surprised that his son, who seems to know nothing about masturbation, nonetheless knows that it isn't allowed and has formed the hypothesis that it's dangerous. Such certainties really go without saying in the system of "freedom" in which this trailblazing dad keeps his happy family... If that freedom weren't pretence, a well-lubricated device for hyper-repression, the dialogue would have been something like:

Jean: So masturbation isn't allowed?

Dad: Why, no, it is. You must have known that since you started jerking off.

Jean: Yes, but there are guys in my class who says that it's bad.

Dad: It's because of their parents, who "often say anything at all." Those children are unhappy.

No. On the contrary, the text reaffirms the prohibition, points out that its previous pretexts are false, then states the "true" reasons for prohibiting jerking off. *If the child gets to like it...*

Obviously there's no guarantee that the child will get to like it. If little Jean had touched himself inadvertently, he would have been so bored, so disappointed (it's not "better" enough), so disgusted that he would have run to take refuge in his mom's arms, sniveling that the nasty thing had bitten him—even that it felt like it was stinging at one point. But alas, other children, snickering friends at school, the "big guys from eighth grade," who have bad parents, aren't so oversensitive: they're "getting to like it." They do it a lot, they flaunt the "practice"; and since twentieth-century-style masturbation no longer rots the spinal cord, even their body doesn't punish them for it.

Fortunately, there's an economic punishment waiting for them. Whereas the well-neutered child keeps his chances of later sampling this pleasure, which is better when it's shared, his chance of making a profitable deal—an investment with a 100% profit yield (pleasure "doubled")—his nasty friends will have nothing: they'll spend their capital like water, and it will be at 0% until they die.

It amazes me that in choosing such an argument to dissuade its readers, this work has unconsciously stated the fundamental law of the sexual market at the center of the ideology that it's defending. But we're dealing with a pedagogy of reward systems, and therefore we must match the prohibition with a reward: castrate yourself and look what you'll get. Who'd refuse to deprive himself of something small (a little pee-pee, a little bit of pleasure for one) in exchange for something big (a good adult body, a good future deal)?

At the same time, the doctors know that among their readers, the organ-vestige has developed quite detached from the body, ready for investment, and that it wants to function; but that it can't, and that pubescent children (12-14) are coming up against a more general prohibition than masturbation. And this, the text is also aware, is being provoked by "sexual destitution." Then how can you distract a child from sexuality, when he's beginning to experience desire as a lack?

Easy enough: you have to tell him, with all the authority of the power of medicine, that "sexual destitution" is an illusion, a disease. A well-balanced child doesn't suffer from it. The muddled theoretical verbiage put in the mouth of the father when he explains why the "big guy from eighth grade" is singing the praises of "pleasure for one" implies that this big guy is unhappy because his parents aren't supervising his neutering.

That's why he's aware of his "sexual destitution" and speaks so highly of masturbation—"merely to protest" this destitution. Protest! Isn't that proof that he's sick? What is this ridiculous demand, this absurd claim? Is he supposed to have a "sex life," then? Doesn't he know that he'd be incapable of managing it properly? Hasn't he read (vol. 7–9 years) that, at *around 18 or 20, adolescents have attained their adult size*—in other words, that even they, who look like adults, are still actually *adolescents*, sexless subhumans? And this thirteen- or fourteen-year-old squirt would like to "put his penis into the vagina of a young girl?" An "anxious" child who went so far as to not even write on the door of his "locker" that he'd like "to have a baby?"

The profound cruelty of medical reasoning is obvious. It tells people who have no freedom to make love that making love is a lot better than masturbating. I have a feeling that they already suspected it. If they had the right to fuck, they wouldn't be reduced by it to the "pleasure" of the "unhappy" children—and all the frustrated people in the world. Prohibiting the only pleasure possible and infusing it with guilt on behalf of what it replaces and is forbidden: such is the revolting practice, the appalling cheat that sex education just invented.

If masturbating until 18 or 20 really does risk putting the sexual appetites of the frustrated off course, I wonder what the complete abstinence advocated by the book will do. Or rather, I know: psychosexual disabilities, panic, impotence, increasingly paralyzed censorship, terror about the body, fear of relating to others, fear of pleasure, fear of "loss," a fanatical desire for jealous, uncompromising private ownership of the sexual object you finally obtain. But all of that is good, even very good: because this is the soil in which the sexual Order takes root.

The child who jerks off is *troubled*, he *becomes anxious*, he *feels abandoned*, loses all interest *in work* and *withdraws more and more*. Translation: the only kind of masturbation among all the childhood and pre-adolescent pleasures "for one" that can cause such a state is a compensatory and guilt-ridden jerking off, a divided, disgusted and ashamed relationship to oneself, the kind of pleasure that submits to all the puritanical restrictions of good sex. This isn't pleasure, but a repressive war between the subject and his organs. Pushed by frustration, he reinforces and internalizes the laws that provoke it. His masturbatory fantasies will portray stereotypes of gratification, a clichéd eroticism, trivial and conformist scenes of pleasure: representational material gleaned from commonplaces promoted by social views of "pleasure." This isn't so much a type of vice as self-bludgeoning indoctrination.

Brief fantasies, embodied by simplistic images of a desire that would quickly outflank received stereotypes if allowed to express itself at that age. It takes many years of masturbation to establish such a "culture" in someone's head, many years of sexual isolation, persistent fear and shame. There will come a time when you will know while having sex how to resist the filthy fancies of certain partners, how to police the bed, control your actions in an orderly way, rectify rituals and rules. On the other hand, even if your desire is clichéd during childhood and adolescence, the clichés are weak and vague, a pure substitute for something that is inapproachable and unknown in its concrete form: as soon discovered as revised.

Through the impossibility of all sexual experience, the preadolescent explores all social experience: he's not wanted anywhere, he exists no more in the eyes of adults than children do in his eyes. No need to list the social virtues of this well-tiered pyramid of contempt.

Being shut up within the family weighs on him. Schoolwork— promotion leading in theory to the status of well-paid producer, purchaser of pleasures forbidden to children—loses all meaning: his reason for being suddenly seems too distant, too unpredictable, compared to the very present and urgent needs that the frustrated person feels and that he now knows how to name.

Does he *feel abandoned*? He sees that the vampirism of school and family, that blood-sucking that he endures day after day, has no compensation (as there is for adult work), that it's a fool's bargain, an exploitation of his body in exchange for which he receives only small, inane, virtuous trinkets. He *withdraws more and more* because he's withdrawing from these deals and there's no way of living from others. Except in crime, which he hesitates to do. The giving-to-get machine that has been constructed on his sex, this libidinal cash register can't function for lack of customers in the shop: the door is locked, the key in Dad's pocket. The merchandising protocol to which he has already become resigned as a means to the appeasement of his desires is unworkable. And he can resort neither to that nor to something else. He's stuck. Does he really have good reason to feel "unhappy" and "troubled"? Why is he being deprived for so long of the pleasure of obeying? He can uphold his end of all the good contracts about which he's been taught, that's what he wants to do. So?

A lot of boys begin to experience this paradoxical situation (revolting out of a need for sexual orthodoxy) around the age of 13 or 14; but it takes shape much earlier, and gradually, the descent occurs step by step—and you almost never come back up. In depicting it the way we have seen, the *Encyclopedia* intends to suggest to its readers that it's their fault if they are subjected to it: the solution is to surrender to your family, school, to submit, to wait. Too bad for those who can no longer bear complying without any result, and who want to exert the full effect of their exasperated conformities on some object. Because having a "complete" body and a standardized desire won't be enough to find acceptance on the sexual market; you must also be worth something on the work market; be economically able to govern, preserve, manage objects of desire. A minor can't be an owner and thus doesn't have what's needed to have sex.

Those whose "sexual destitution" interferes with their blindly optimistic slavery, those who are malcontent jerk-offs who envy the middle class person and his middle classes, instead of being "fully developed high school students," inspire no compassion and have no excuse. There are no doubts about their morals but there are suspicions about these breaking down without some good prisons to protect them: marriage, children, work, home—and they won't have a right to these until much later. While waiting, then, they must content themselves with those in which they are.

But they are making them unhappy? An unjustifiable feeling, which prepares them for worse misfortune; and just round the bend psychiatry is waiting—for the first appearance of an idiosyncrasy: open fly, lack of discipline, "academic maladjustment," circles too dark under the eyes, subversive ideas, sullen participation in family life, not to mention the big crimes: fornication, attempts at suicide, delinquency and perversion.

After having spit in the face of the frustrated and not very submissive, our doctors have one more duty to fulfill: warning other children about bad associations.

Because shackled as the child is, there are still two things that can jeopardize his complete castration: contact with poorly neutered associates at school and with strangers in the street.

"Perverted" high schoolers are rarely content with modestly writing: *Hurray for pleasure for one.* They'd rather make sure that it's no longer for one at all. Even if it is "hard to love someone else," the age at which loving is prohibited is the one when you share your pleasures more readily than you do later on.

Except with those kids who are ultracensored, of course. They're already saving themselves up: when you have a good-looking face, nice clothes, a middle class family, a big apartment, you know you're worth a lot and you don't associate with inferiors whose bodies happen to be freer, and who deprivatize that much more willingly since they have nothing to "lose." Conversion of every young member of the middle class into an aggressive, cowardly self-infatuated little big-person, who is impatient to consume, buy, show his power, protects him quite effectively from the "vice" that would compromise the respectable façade that little boys and girls want to affect, and would represent a sacrilegious squandering for people already concerned with savings and profit. If children "mature" earlier than they used to (without taking into account physical precocity), it's simply because they quickly start copying the putrid pretense, greediness, spirit of servility, hateful aloofness of the typical French status-seeker. Verifying whether there are any secret relapses from this imitation of adult degradation would be the province of a kind of ethnology that doesn't exist.

In any case, the authors of the *Encyclopedia* who (like all educators) are busy piling up the safeguards around the minor seem to believe that such secret erotism always exists; their dissuading arguments aim for two opposing, complementary poles. On the one hand, make tomorrow's victims of exploitation submit to the order and believe they have a stake in it. On the other, properly disconcert the spirit of children who really do have a stake in respecting this order: for they are the sons and daughters of the bourgeoisie who will receive the Heritage. The preservation of the family depends upon obedience to the economic schemas of marketable sexuality: and the family must be perpetuated because it alone maintains both the servitude of the greatest number and the power of the elite. I'd like to see the day when a few perverted kids go around teaching that you can have an orgasm without a contract, suddenly unhinging the brains of the heirs and their future flock.

What's surprising about education's rabid opposition to the erotism of minors is that the latter itself doesn't interfere with anything, and that far from being at odds with the sexual order, it embodies several parodic but faithful applications of it. Such amusements have never changed the path of many people—just think how they thrived during a time when children weren't "informed," and keep in mind that they certainly didn't alter our contemporaries' charmingly harsh morals (cf. the *Simon Report* on—appropriately—the asexuality of the French).

But there's a difference between then and now, and it's considerable: nothing can be instilled with enough guilt any more. Censorship is weakening, prohibitions giving way, each chooses his own taboos in the name of desire itself, we no longer know to which repression to devote ourselves in order to be happy.

And this means that the minor's pleasures—formerly lived in the face of such shame that he forgot them forever starting with the age of the contract—could henceforth be sampled without distress and would very soon trouble the adult order. Among our parents, there are a great many of the most puritanical fathers who nevertheless spent their studious adolescence jerking off like wild men, sucking cocks, fucking clever, well-made-up great-grandmothers, or letting themselves be buggered out of appetite, interest or a respect for values. I myself know a few of them among the people my age. Then they cleaned up their act, censored it, forgot it; they can never be made to admit it—unless they pose as criminals who've been redeemed to better condemn those who are doing the same thing they did. But generally, only their less shamed and less prudish partners remember, with amusement or even with pleasure. What begets the order, then, depends not only on whether you've tasted a pleasure or not, it's that you feel so deeply guilty about it that you'll relinquish it as soon as you move on to those that the order approves.

The old Christian morality instilled guilt admirably; the new law—obeying-equals-the-right-to-come—is at least as reliable. Betting on both horses—the pressures of the duty to make a profit and the residue of shame—will become the art of repression French-style for this fine quarter of the century. Conservative doctors observe the agonies of the old order and have discovered, they hope, the medicine that will save the life of this valuable patient with whom the middle class have entrusted them: snuff out the evil at its root and, combining the task of informing with the mission of prohibiting, dive for the throats of pleasures that were once only shameful games favorable to the order but that now risk leading to freedom itself.

What are these household or high school games that make them so indignant? First of all, you rarely write on doors, and certainly not in that kind of language. You'd rather talk, draw—and something other than ovaries. You jerk off in front of others, or in pairs, or in threes or more. And that's not everyday, nor as a rule. You tell stories, make things up, poke around, compare, you're curious about those who have jism, you talk about the opposite sex and get busy with our own, you have a vague desire to stick it in something, which sometimes takes shape and finds its accomplice, or star, or victim. Poor little Jean, for example, with his long pretty hair, his stupid manner, his nice medical *penis*, obstinately and *completely limp*, and his mom who tells him that from the back he looks like his sister… *Boy or girl, what's the difference?* is Sylvie's point of view. The women in the family certainly have embarrassing opinions if a "big guy from eighth grade" in the "locker room" decides to take them at their word.

What doesn't exist, isn't named—is it allowed or prohibited? Because the Book doesn't talk about the anus. Can it, too, be used to *share*, to make things *double*?

Certainly seems to, tsk, tsk. It's just like Dad-Mom. Jean notices, his conscience at peace, that *the penis in erection slips inside* him *instinctively*—ouch!—and that *the two bodies become no more than one.* They *find a movement together*—yeah, keep goin'!—*and the pleasure that both of them are feeling is so strong that the man* (sorry, the big guy from eighth grade) *has an ejaculation.* It certainly is *orgasm*, even though Jean was getting hard—which worries him: getting a hard-on standing on two feet in broad daylight is impossible, according to his book; so does *orgasm* make you sleepwalk? But wait, he feels just like he's woken up. Strange. Let's hope it's not a disease, getting a hard-on deliberately and when the sun is out… In fact, everything went according to the rules, except they didn't *feel wonderfully peaceful together*, because math class was starting.

Jean will come home feeling perplexed. The problem is that even if *the spurt* was *powerful enough*, no *sperm* would have been able *to reach the ovum*. But wouldn't that be *how*, for example, *you can—if you want*, not to *have a baby?* It must work that way sometimes.

And this is serious: certainly this is the moment when *Dad, very moved, squeezes Mom's hand* (as he did at the concert, when she was pregnant and Jean moved inside her belly) because—ouch!—it actually does hurt a little. The resemblance between being pregnant and being fucked in the ass is disconcerting: the same words are used to describe every kind of pleasure, that must be why. With Jean as well, earlier, someone *squeezed* him *hard, very hard, looked* at him, *very moved*, and someone *moved inside him for the first time*—it wasn't a baby, moreover, ouch no. All that was missing was some Mozart. Jean scrubbed his ass pensively: is this what they call *a feeling of total fulfillment?* First of all, does a boy have the right to feel completely full? He'll have to *reread the book with dad*, there are some things that he must have misunderstood.[10]

Sodomy or not, initiation or not, co-ed school, girls' school or boys', all the dangers of promiscuity—a scrambling of the "good" code—prowl around a child as soon as he leaves the family nest and finds himself among his peers. Just imagine that a "big guy" lends his book to the "little guys," imagine that secondary school sex education trickles down to the primary grades through the intermediary of the "locker room." It would be one of the least obligations of student solidarity. But what's the use of their having so skillfully written each volume, their having falsified information, pulled off their fraud, censored, deceived, frightened, sickened? Imagine that some cute little detail removed from the book gets around, and the construct of lies in which preadolescents were being ensnared will be dashed to pieces.

All the efficiency of indoctrination is due on one hand to the impossibility of experiencing a desire freely during the years when that freedom would undermine our rickety codes and our quaint

---

10. Obviously I wanted to say that many homosexual amusements at that age are as normative as they come, conforming to conjugal orthodoxy, to its inequalities and restrictions. Moreover, homosexuality in itself is not always exempt from this.

As for the shocking comparison between buggery and being pregnant, it goes without saying that as soon as the pleasure of having a cock inside your body stops being depreciated, the honor of having a fetus there won't be overemphasized. And it isn't my fault if the *Encyclopedia* repeats in every manner that the thrills of pregnancy are due to the presence of a little male who is "moving" inside a woman. Jean's exclamation—*he'll play rugby!*—has what it takes to awaken in the ladies some very appealing fantasies (cf. the female public hysteria at sports events), and in certain homosexuals as well, of course. Not to mention the fathers themselves...

prohibitions; and on the other, to non-communication among minors. The first is acquired, because society sees to it, but the second?

Can one count absolutely on the segregations that already exist and that are taught and reinforced by adults? Little children spurned by bigger ones, preadolescents spurned by adolescents, who are in turn spurned by young people getting out of school. (If you want to transform an antiestablishment type of 18–20 into a conscientious and even often brutal junior cop, put a gang of 12- or 14-year-old children into his clutches—cf. summer camp, boarding school, etc. We hate being subjected to one form of order and love inflicting another form on others. And that's why it's enough to grant a smidgen of official power to a rebel to change him into a flunkey. The formula is as old as time itself.)

Segregation between rich and poor children, middle class and technical-school students, girls and boys, the strong and the weak, fat and thin, foreigner and French, etc. Everything that differentiates serves to generate inequality, build hierarchy, separate; and contacts among children for the most part respect social communities established by adults.

In despite of this, minors are still somewhat capable of speaking to each other on a superficial level, associating ritually and—all economic divides and all types of racism taken into account—getting along with each other well enough. That survival of civilization, of sociability intensely displeases parents, who endeavor to put an end to it by controlling the friendships of their offspring, limiting their going out, selecting and directing their leisure activities. Without school, we'd be at the point at which children, adolescents no longer met one another except when they went out into the street, each of them held by hand or by word, nondetachable from dad-mom; and they would exchange startled looks from afar, the way a dog on a leash extends its muzzle toward another dog on a leash when two ladies-who-love-dogs walk cantankerously past one another on the same sidewalk. The nuclear family on the prowl, tense, anxious and huddled together like the old comic-strip family, the Fenouillards, out tiger-hunting, is already a common site on our quietest streets. We also know that such outrageous privatization of childhood is particularly French. Only the middle class is economically sound enough to practice it rigorously; but it is the family ideal of the other classes, whose lack of money, time and space doesn't allow them to devote themselves to it as perfectly.

Consequently, what remains of the child's life in society can compromise the long and patient internalization of the propaganda. Solution: any noninstitutional relations will be prohibited; they should walk around with a sign on their stomach: Attention: freshly censored, do not touch.

It's disturbing that the barrier "protecting" childhood actually resembles the fence around a demolition site.

When it comes to promiscuity and children, the *Encyclopedia* has had the courage to go quite far in anticipating the dangers of brainwashing for which it can put you at risk. But decency limits this virtuous daring; and for lack of being able really to penetrate the secretiveness of the world of "minors," it is reduced to brandishing the specter of it to prevent the child from taking refuge in it. He must fear or hate bad companions, see in each child who is free or "different" someone who is sick, in each unknown adult a dangerous nut; must receive not a shred of uncontrolled information without showing it immediately to Dad; he must sur-privatize, go everywhere with his family ahead of him, as if surrounded by an invisible cord cordon from the riot squad; and finally, he must be afraid, afraid, afraid and afraid.

We may now summarize this state-of-the-art technique of castration. Take hold of the child very gently, quietly, amuse him with images, tell him some tall stories, keep him from tensing up, encourage him very patiently to open his thighs, increase the "cuddles" to reassure him—suddenly grab his dick and tear it off with a sharp movement.

Explain to him that like that he'll be happy from now on; and as proof show him the hell he's escaping. Here it is:

I admit that this photo disturbed me the first time I saw it in the handbook for 10–13-year-olds. No matter how well I knew that neither decorated doctors, parents of schoolchildren nor homosexuals-who-want-to-marry-before-God have little liking for pedophiles (who do so much harm to these three worthy social categories), I never would have expected that in 1973 we'd dig up such an old scarecrow, a boogeyman so moth-eaten and pathetic. Maybe it will become a sign of the endearing period that produced the mentality of those who are reviving it, for the edification of today's children. But of course, Dad believes in it.

In any case, if this image doesn't represent any real human being, it still has some reality in the "collective unconscious" of the middle class: because it personifies Evil, Sex and the Other. I'd believed that this trinity of a god-demon was dead—but yet again, what the priests have abandoned, medicine hangs on to.

We are at the end of the book, at the moment of the great putting on guard that follows all lessons in French liberty. Immediately after the condemnation of the masturbatory 0%, and before the book concludes with the happiness of the family (running wildly in the fields, a double-page photo): *They have put down the book, and all four have gone to feel the cool grass under their bare feet. Turn the page and see their joy!* In passing, we will make note of this eulogy to an elitist pleasure: for middle class people who have some grass in the country are the same ones who prohibit less lucky children with or without shoes who don't leave the city from walking on the lawns of public parks. Can't they understand that happiness isn't trampling the grass that you find but working well and obeying well so that you can buy some for yourself and surround it with a lovely picket fence?

I had the feeling that this succession of images, the-horrible-man-in-the-park-tragedy and the well-neutered-family-happiness had something tendentious about it. It resembled the other complex of information: contraception-nasty-condom preceding the avalanche of lovely babies and the long dialogues about pregnancy-reward. All in all, it seemed as if it were proving a bit too well, and even a little too much, that sex education doesn't exactly have the intentions it claims to, but rather those I was saying it has. The text that accompanies the horrible photo, and which I will barely comment upon, passes onto some full confessions. See for yourself:

Dad searches the two young faces as if he were trying to guess something. Then he quietly asks a burning question:

"Have you already encountered any exhibitionists?"

"Any what?"

"Men who hang around primary schools and high schools, for example, and show their penis by sneakily and a bit shamefully opening their coat." Jean nods:

"I saw one in the park. I got scared and looked away. I was all alone and he hid himself before showing his open fly. Is it a sickness?"

"These men aren't dangerous. They obviously had some problems when they were children. But no one noticed and tried to understand them... So their sexuality never reached a normal stage, and later they do this to get even. They target children. Probably the fear that you felt gave him a little pleasure. That's all."

"He wouldn't have ever tried to touch me?"

"Definitely not. But there are other sexually sick people who are very dangerous, and since you're children, you can't identify them. They're 'sadists,' who sometimes feel a horrible need to harm little boys or little girls. Those are the ones who speak to children, offer them presents, candy, ice cream, toys, to attract them. You must never go with an unknown person who's being extremely nice. It's a trap. If he insists and comes after you: shout, call for help. People will understand immediately without your having to explain the situation. Besides, those kind of men are always very cowardly and run away at your first call."

How do pedophiles cope in a country where having sex with consenting minors (whether they're ten or sixteen)[11] leads to prison? If they're rich, it's very simple: they wait patiently for their vacations and indulge in a very thriving pedophiliac sex tourism, for which vacation clubs and travel agents are glad to serve them: Mediterranean countries in Europe or Africa, the Middle East, South America, India, Pakistan, noncommunist countries in Asia, etc. The geography of the permitted is at least as vast as that of the prohibited, the laws or customs that specify minimum age vary incredibly from one place to another, the pedophilias of custom, religion, hospitality or prostitution are combined, and what will get you lynched in one place wins you a fond smile from parents elsewhere. Therefore pedophiles, who are *always very cowardly, run away* on the *first* plane that will take them to a tolerant country. Good riddance, but the worst ones are still around: the ones who are broke.

These are the "danger," whose story Dad just told—by concealing their multitude beneath two dreadful masks: the-man-who-shows and the man-who-kills. It isn't a matter of pederasts themselves in the father's tale because he'd only be able to say one thing about them: they like to have sex with you and you shouldn't have sex with them—nor with anyone.

And the liberal's discourse would have at least to justify such a prohibition, and that would engender a flood of questions and answers that would reveal everything that has been censored on page after page on behalf of the pro-birth stance and the castration of children.

---

11. It should be pointed out that among pubescent and prepubescent children, there is no difference in *capacity* for pleasure; all that changes, more or less, is the acting out of this pleasure, its codes, its roles, its socialization.

Because the prohibition that strikes a blow against pederasty is a simple corollary to the one in this country that condemns both homosexuality and the sexuality of minors, it's also a corollary of the law that gives parents the ownership and exclusive utilization of their progeny. If the pedophile is the object of the most violent repression, the fiercest condemnation, it's because he violates these three assumptions that are at the basis of our entire sexual order. Consequently, those homosexuals who want to win acceptance exonerate themselves from being pederasts and denounce them as the only "real" perverts; adolescents who want the right to love solemnly vow to interest themselves only in conjugal pleasures; and as for the parents, they're prohibiting incest or at least getting credited for it in advance.

Training for the sexual order means implanting these three principles in children. It's impossible to name, honestly depict a forbidden sexuality, which would reveal that only arbitrary social powers have created laws that are being attributed to nature—a sexuality that, in addition (I'll come back to this later), has the peculiarity of very often and to the letter exploiting the patterns of marketable sexuality and the mechanisms of parental power—in other words, the very indoctrination of the child and the details of his status. The pedophile goes beyond being simply a pervert, a squanderer: he's the father's rival. Nothing is closer to the Order, and it has no greater enemy; hardly have we mentioned the pedophile before we're already dissecting the parent-child relationship. Jean's dad narrowly misses that pitfall when he says that the *niceness* of the pedophile is *a trap*: a lot of children already know that when it comes to adults (parents, teachers or managers) being *extremely nice* almost always hides a dirty trick about to be played on you. Will they guess that the *niceness* of the authors of the *Encyclopedia* is also hiding *a trap*, and that it goes way beyond those we'd imagined being offered children?

Keep quiet about pedophilia and yet ward off its "threat"; through it, fix in your sights any inclination toward emancipation on the part of the minor: that's what the big man in the black raincoat, this sad old guy dressed like a poor person, is for—this pitiful state of Temptation, well designed to disgust the child enough to keep him from ever succumbing. So that's what having a sexuality is? So it's not being like everybody else? That's pleasure? When you desire, that's what you look like? When you're desired, that's what you're subjected to? Disobeying your parents means becoming that? Going out to the street, being outside, being alone and free means meeting that? When an adult is interested in children it's to *get even?* Behind all the boys, girls, all the people who speak to me, behind all the passersby Outside, all the ones who don't walk quickly by ignoring me, this is what there is?

A lovely lesson, to be sure, that will certainly help children *avoid unpleasant surprises,* and make *the sex life* a *terrible secret* or *a mystery* for them.

I fear, however, that the buckle of fear may be forever buckled and that, may I add, the *mystery* closes over this coat that is opening. And I wonder how many well-neutered children sent on the run by an exhibitionist will only have been fleeing their own future. Terror lasts, in the same way for the child feeling guilty for having seen as for the old guy feeling guilty for having shown; and the former has to be the surest path to the latter. Because only one system for seeing a penis can terrify and traumatize the child: the one of total prohibition and absolute culpability.

Let's admire the two faces of the poor man, the two "monsters" that will instill horror where there is none: the Exhibitionist, who gets "a little pleasure" from making the child feel *fear,* and the Sadist who has "a need to harm him."

In truth, sadists, child killer-torturers are extremely rare; the law practically never gets hold of them, and family journalism, which loves dismemberment, resigns itself to raking through the five continents to offer its readers one or two per year. A necessary task: it upholds the family myth of the Stranger, of the Man-Who-Kills, so that the image of sadism can do an impeccable job of covering over that of the pedophile, and so that, in current parlance, the word "sadist" can serve to indicate any caresser of little girls or boys— except for old grannies.

As for exhibitionists, despite my many walks in parks, I've never seen one at work: guess I'm too old. In any case, and Dad himself admits it, they're *inoffensive*.

However, lets remove these two masks and remind ourselves what they're hiding: pederasts looking for young boys in order to have sex with them, for a quickie or also involving friendship.

Looking for consenting minors involves some frightful practices: you have to "speak to children" and even be "extremely nice," because "unknown people" always frighten them. Actually, pedophiles only "attract" boys who are free with themselves and who are interested in it. When it's a matter of a mutual itch, you understand each other quickly, and if you don't, you say hello.

I haven't yet read about a rejected queer starting to "follow" the child while polishing his big knife. Sometimes he insists? If there were no "mystery" in morals, no panic, no risk of prison, but legitimate information, in this case, an invitation, the response could be expressed clearly, openly, without insisting and without anxiety. But in our society, when an adult encounters a child, two fears come to the fore—and the most terrifying one isn't what you think.

For such a search entails innumerable difficulties: cruising is a primitive state—excuse me, I mean it's "crime" on the prowl. *Hanging around primary schools and high schools*, and in the streets, swimming pools, parks, train stations, movie theaters, at urinals: wherever outsiders of every shape and kind spontaneously gather. A wearing form of survival for some, a dangerous, embittered existence. I've already described how the bourgeois pedophile avoids it.

In addition, you wriggle out of it at the bottom—among the humiliated, the poor, the unsightly, the shy—by sneaking away. You succumb to fear, omnipresent physical fear. After thirty or fifty years of frustration, anxiety, you make yourself some armor (the black coat): self-punishment, guilt, self-loathing. Desire changes into torment, you're condemned to awkward, panicked, pathetic "acting out"—for example, exhibitionism. An acting out that is so unrealistic that it soon lands you in the hands of nice people and the cops.

No need for the child to *explain the situation*: it is very true that passersby *understand immediately*. They understand that they're getting the ideal victim, the perfect monster, the one whose hand kills as soon as it touches. According to the contemporary sexual order, this dangerous crazy is exactly the same thing as the nineteenth-century bourgeois order's stealer of bread: the absolute criminal, the man to bring down. That isn't what the law stipulates, but honest folks' "understanding" is unanimous about it. Those who live to walk all over people, strangle children and exploit inequality to the point of drawing blood are actually outraged that such people would dare "go after somebody weaker than them."

Such childish "weakness" is highly valued: the fangs and claws of twenty million adults are spiking from every inch of its skin, and whoever touches it immediately risks his own. No wonder why the faggot takes off if the "victim" calls out. That flight proves that he's *cowardly* and that he has criminal intentions—if not he would have stuck around to quietly explain the situation to the nice witnesses, to be sure.

Sexuality that has, as Dad says, *never reached a normal stage*: it tears itself apart a little more as each year passes, and it doesn't "develop" very much. Instead of feeling sorry for "perverts" that no one *tried to understand* when they were children, it would be better to point out that everyone is determined to crush them once they're adults. In my opinion, the latter is the decisive factor. But Dad and I aren't on the same wavelength: he meant that a well-adjusted child doesn't become a pervert. "Perversion," then, the refusal of an arbitrary sexual order, will only be a very regrettable disease. And psycho-whatevers will cheerfully draw up an inventory—in the spirit of a mythical "scientific" good conscience—of the behavioral disturbances, the manias, the failures, the neuroses that a life of loneliness and persecution causes the deviant, and that proves his "disease." The most surprising thing about it is that most of the outlaws endure, and aren't destroyed by, a sexual and social system that would drive the majority of "normal" people to suicide or an asylum after just a few weeks.

Rich perverts and poor perverts aren't at all the same thing; all freedoms can be bought, and so can this one, but it costs a little more.

Between the options of the powerful and the setbacks of poverty, petit bourgeois pederasts find an institutional refuge in professions offering power over childhood. Primary high school teaching, the priesthood, there's a choice. They represent the parents, they divert their power, hide behind it, they fashion a weapon out of it and the kid can only submit. They are the Order.

That fashion of surviving is especially odious, because of the collaboration it implies and the coercion it inflicts upon the child-object, while taking advantage of the status and rights it receives from the family. Of course, it's no more disgusting than any other absue in the name of any other desire. An institutional relationship to the child allows this kind of queer to avoid illegal cruising and pitiful seduction scenes. He's aware that you can't attract a child by showing him what he has learned to fear the most. The action of showing was replacing that of touching, it was like a preliminary for it that is discontinued, a pawing of the ground, a reversion, a kind of rehabilitated gesture, a way to redeem a desire eating away at you, a way to live it differently. The pederast-educator figures out that children are much less taken aback by being touched: they know what that is, and a lot of them are hardly alarmed by it. If you want to be privatized, you always give in to Dad—I mean, to the Power with a hundred heads, the law of the strongest. Kids are used to higher authorities—adults—fondling them for any pretext at all, from their little familial spankings to the tugging of their medical balls; the teach's, priest's hand will only be one more grope, it's the life of the slave.

Dad doesn't use his fingers, that's what distinguishes him from pederast-educators: he has an iron or velvet glove, but it's a glove. We saw Jean bare-naked with his dad bare-naked, and they were talking about somebody showing his little thing; it was this "innocent" context "without shame" that made the conversation so amusing. Jean was saying that he was *scared to look at a penis* and he *looked away*. What did he see? An open fly; in other words, crime. What does he see at home? Dad without his pants; in other words, law. An unknown person has been deprivatized, "divulged" for him—and Jean was afraid of being touched, as if that were the logical consequence of it.

The deprivatization of the man seemed to call for that of the child—who has learned not to be deprivatized except within his family, in an asexual context. Father and son, naked in front of each other, have no genitals for each other; and when Jean sees his dad's cock, he doesn't need to look away, because there's nothing to see. The stranger is dad without that cancellation.

Even comparing the photos is meaningful. Within the family, Jean looks at the faces of those who are naked. In the park, Jean ignores the face of the dressed gentleman, but stares at his fly.

In his former soldier's cap, the old man in the park is nothing other than a statue of parental power. He incarnates its cruelty and reveals paradoxically what's at stake in it. The fear that he inspires is felt by any child in front of adults who break their own laws, such as he has learned them.

And first in front of his parents. At home, coexistence is based on strict rules, skillful submissions, calculations, little daily deals. But everything can explode at any time, and his parents transform into wild beasts from whom there is no escape. Dad-Mom, as punishers or furies, suddenly become people who take "a little pleasure" in causing fear, who "get even," and who have a "horrible need to harm little boys or little girls." Nearly all children have experienced such sadism; and the boogeyman is—much more than outside strangers—that stranger lurking inside the father, who makes a monstrous appearance from time to time. But the child subjected to such family violence can't *shout, call for help*: papa exercises his power, and there's no getting away from it.

This is where the man in the black coat achieves his true reality. A pathetic addition to parental abuse, he becomes the symbol of it in the child's imagination. You run away from him as you'd like to run away from the father; only a few children are sometimes fascinated by him—less out of confidence than out of excess of submission. And the reason that the father puts them on guard against these men is because these false images-to-obey resemble him. *Since you're children, you can't identify them*: what he wants to say is that there are dads everywhere giving out toys, presents, candy, who invite you into their car; careful, these are booby-trapped dads. The only good one is me.

But the child who has the best chance of remembering such a warning, the most ignorant child, the most docile (for example, Jean), is also the one that men-like-dad will catch in the "trap" by showing that they're not mean like Dad is. Whereas the children who distrust adults, detest Dad and are rearing under the yoke (like the "big guy from eighth grade") are the ones who shrug and keep walking when an adult whom they don't like bothers them.

Yes, that's what I said: whom they don't like. This is what bothers the families. Runaways quickly discover that the outside is full of refuges and inhabited by detestable or likeable human beings who aren't dangerous, and certain of whom can play the role of parents. The middle class pederast will be as usable as a father, and according to a similar deal: to buy his protection, the children or adolescents will have to give in to him, submit their sex to him, as they do for the father; but instead of being castrated, they'll only be harnessed, and will have to live dependant rather than as someone quashed. The sexual rivalry between parents and pederasts represents the alternation between two options for a child's domestic survival. In countries where pederasty is tolerated, the wealthy queer, whether he be a tourist or not, in a poor boy's eyes becomes the economic complement of parents, the one who might extract him from a life without future, from an otherwise irremediable destitution; the one who'll pay for his studies and make him... a father of a middle class family. To put it briefly, the homosexual protector offers, outside the family, what that family can't give. It's no longer a question of each according to his birth, but of each according to his pretty face. It's not that different, in fact it's altogether the same—but it's in addition.

In our country, this normalizing and family-centricizing economic role also exists, but much more secretly. Boys who have "uncles" so that they can one day be fathers are more numerous than you think.

It's clear that pederasties that have made a pact with the Order are as varied as possible; and as long as a pederast has power, money and knows how to respect middle class values and manipulate with them, he'll do quite well.

There are still, as I've mentioned, the poor, the dissident, the cruisers—and the young, because you can be a "pedophile" at twelve, sixteen or twenty as well as you can be one at sixty. They don't have the means, the need, the desire to collude. There will be simple communication with the child through desire, reciprocal desire. Does this exist? Yes, and educators know it. Because such pederasty lacks the terrifying face of parental power, in a black coat or a pair of drawers made of human skin; it's not a trick, a form of abuse, and it preserves only the initial accord from the patterns of the sexual market; it lives, only and directly, from what the parents condemn, from what a lot of children deny themselves, from what self-righteous pederasts coat with social bonuses, the conjugal and family-centrism: pleasure. It exists at the meeting point of two rebellions, two desires usually deflected by the family order that is formed by the couples: desire of the child for the adult and desire of the adult for the child. Very "temporary" couples: sexualities of expenditure have no tomorrow—tomorrow, in this society, is always the beginning of the order, the opening of a market, a deal for pleasure that becomes a contract of exploitation.

You can't warn children against that "danger." We know that they're involved in it by their own choice and if, outside, what resembles dad frightens them, what doesn't resemble him seduces them too often. We don't dare show, photograph a "danger" that doesn't have a father's face: no child would be able to find it threatening. So we use the image of a dreadful father to stigmatize his opposite; and to dissuade a child from heeding a desire, we need do nothing more than put him on guard against humanity in general.

Don't accept candy, presents, don't speak to anyone, don't hang around, don't listen, don't look, don't get into a man's car, it's dangerous: when you're outside, everyone wants to kill you, O.K.? Kill you.

Certainly it's reasonable for parents to caution their children about not getting into cars; but I think that they're mistaken about the reason. They're afraid that the child will fall into the hands of a "maniac," who'll touch him, show himself and God knows what else. The risk is low, and incidents are slight. The real danger about the invitation to get into the car is an accident on the road. There's something criminal about transporting a child in an automobile; you immediately expose him to wounds, mutilation, permanent disability and death. France's millions of alcoholics aren't the ones who will argue about that. But such industrial cruelty is legal, whereas the sexual pseudo-misdeeds are condemned. I'm not trying to justify these "misdeeds," which are absolutely repugnant as abuses of power—and only to the extent that they are, this goes without saying. But on the one hand, it should be pointed out that such abuses exactly match the logic of all relations organized by our society between adults and children, adults and adults, children and children, men and women, etc.; and it certainly would be surprising if people abstained from the only small disgrace that is displeasing to the Order. On the other hand, it surprises me that parents protect their brat from this small form of abuse only to inflict a worse one on him. What they're really trying to protect isn't the child, but their own exclusive right to do whatever they want with him.

In the end, cars and the families who shut themselves up in them are products of the same society of exploitation; the fact that the latter kill themselves with the help of the former thus seems inevitable, if not heartening. Or rather, such "auto-destruction" would be an advantage if it could be used against the social order; but it's still not relentless enough, and the number of families torn to pieces, children reduced to a pulp and automobiles turned into accordions remains too low to impress a public that cheerfully consumes as many horrible news items as they do smarmy novels. To the point that those who survive an accident are in a hurry to buy another car and, after a delay, shut up a new wife and children in it; like those lizards whose tail grows back if it's broken off, in order to be men they tirelessly reproduce these superfluous, fragile, more or less uncooperative accessories that the market of sex and sheet metal offers to their greed.

Enough with the jokes. Each year in West Germany, there are 9,000 children murdered by their own parents. *Equivalent statistics have been gathered in other European countries or the United States, and could be adjusted for France.*[12] These are not, may I point out, accidents on the road, but deaths following physical abuse rained down upon their precious blond heads by dads and moms.

Death in this case is only an exception, a regrettable incident, coming from sudden bad luck during or following an everyday carefree pleasure that is usually without consequence: persecuting children. A practice whose frequency can't be calculated—in so much as that *for a long time doctors have shown the greatest reticence in admitting the existence of abuse committed by the parents themselves.*[13] That's the main reason why we still don't have complete information about parental sadism in France. Medicine only began to describe the "battered-child syndrome," to keep patient charts showing abuse,

---

12. *Le Figaro*, July 23, 1973.

13. ibid.

or, rather, traces of it, in 1962; first in the United States, of course, and today in our country. I wonder how the doctors of the past interpreted those "bruises, hematomas, cuts, burns, multiple wounds" found on young children—an excess of masturbation, no doubt.

The enormous number of deaths, and the immensity of the universe of family-torture implicated by them was mentioned at U.N.E.S.C.O. in July 1973, during the first meeting of the association known as Filium, which brought together pediatricians, sociologists, criminologists and other notables from a variety of nations and was assigned the task of *studying all forms of crimes or offenses committed against children, from physical punishment to extermination by war—abandonment included.*[14]

Thus, parents head the list of criminals, as they should; note, incidentally, that the men-in-the-park don't make the list at all. An unfortunate oversight but, I suppose, temporary.

It is clear, nevertheless, that our notables are sensitive only to traditional genocide. Forms of violence that don't kill attract them as well: "burns from cigarettes, pokers or irons," for example, or "bleeding in the cranium." And they are even interested in the most minute of problems: "clinical indications of malnutrition, emotional deprivation, psychological distress." Aren't poorly mothered little fly-openers classed among those victims? Not a word about it; another peculiar oversight.

As for calling "criminal" the abandonment of kids, who are taken in by institutions, orphanages, etc., which supposedly "contribute in their own way to the destruction of our children" (Professor Rascowsky), this is coming from the scoffers. Finally, to think that a custom as universally appreciated as war—our most

---

14. *Le Monde*, July 20, 1973.

beautiful and costliest proof of civilization, scientific genius and industrial prosperity—is a way for adults of "sending the youngest to be killed on battlefields" really borders on the revolutionary, pacifism and other infantile diseases that psychiatry knows perfectly well how to take care of.

Of course, the members of the Filium association have virtuous intentions; they are careful not to implicate the family or to commit to any political reflection regarding these problems; they only denounce the shortcomings of the order in the name of the order itself, and here we are dealing with a new wave of the very old philanthropic bourgeoisie. Condemning "filicide," they simply mean: today's parents do a bad job at consuming their children. Families must learn to hull their children's brains without shattering the shell, and to impose the order without prematurely killing the producers that it must enslave.

Who are these inept parents? I will draw from a few sources about them from an author who can hardly be suspected of being left wing, Doctor Friedrich Hacker.[15] It will confirm the obvious: the persecution of children is carried out in the name of the Order and it is oedipal. It represents the last word in family life, it's no fantasy.

-----

15. *Agression/violence dans le monde moderne* (Agression/Violence in the Modern World), Calmann-Lévy, 1972. Doctor Hacker claims to have democratic convictions, faith in the saving power of science, Christian humanism full of emotion about the suffering of humanity in prey to violence. Thus he makes an expert psychiatrist for American federal courts, which means that he helps determine whether a criminal should be sentenced to electroshock or the electric chair, to a cell in an asylum or the gas chamber.

He also tells about having put his talents at the service of the police in order to help them identify, uncover and arrest certain psychotic criminals whose idiosyncrasies put cops off the track.

Because children were whining, they have been doused with boiling water, put on a hot stove, been strangled until they die, thrashed until blood flows and their skin is in shreds... Neighbors have heard the sobs, the cries of rage, the heavy blows, the groans followed by silence. But you don't get mixed up in other people's personal business, and these "neighbors" don't intervene, *they approve of and allow the physical abuse,* and *close their ears to the outrage*: it's *impossible*, these tortures, the torturers *must be aware of what they're doing and why.* Doctor Hacker states that 20% of cases of *seriously mistreated children* registered in Los Angeles *resulted in the death of the victim*; he doesn't specify the level of abuse that is considered by a hospital to classify a child as belonging to the statistical category of "seriously mistreated." But a death rate of 20% leaves us to believe that such bad treatment must be fairly extreme; the competition for a place in the statistics is rough.

Doctor Hacker admits that, given the material, the figures *have little meaning: actual proportion of battered children in cities is 10 to 15 times greater than that specified by the statistics. Underestimation of the phenomenon in rural areas could amount to 100 to 200. No other criminal statistic entails such a margin of error.*

Then follows a study done in Los Angeles. Parents who tortured were examined (for a very rare case in which the abuse was reported and the kid taken to the hospital) and found to be *sane*; less than 1% present *any signs of insanity,* and only *1.5% can be classified as sadists, even in the general sense of the word* (the more generalized statistics from Filim confirm 3% to be "mentally ill"). Sixty percent enjoy an income that is higher than average, 40% have an income that is lower. *There is no statistically valid relationship* between this crime and *level of culture, profession, race, religion or the sex* of the parents. Main perpetrator of the persecution, the father, *almost always under the direction of the mother,* women are less likely to pitch in, but *they are worse.*

The environment of the family is *stable,* the number of divorces *does not exceed the average.* The average age of the persecutors is between 20 and 30, that of victims always less than 4 (from 1 to 4 years old: 75%).

For 90% of the parents, the *determining cause of the abuse* was *the tears and incessant screams of the child.* Anger or parental exasperation? No: *a methodical system of cold or cool violence, unaccompanied by emotive hostility, simply practical and reality-based.* It's a matter of maintaining order every day, relentlessly. During family holidays, when nothing must disturb the ritual, *the result of a forced harmony,* there is more beating: *in many pediatric hospitals and clinics there is a noticeable influx of battered children around Christmas. The emotional and solemn atmosphere proves to be particularly intolerant* of any irregularity in the behavior of children. The Christmas tree and the clean carpet are the latest gods to which kids are sacrificed: the child is beaten, killed because *he's crying, dirtying the lovingly cleaned apartment, and shows neither consideration nor respect nor deference.* Most of the time, the persecuted child was *wanted,* but once born, he has *disappointed,* as a source of dirtiness, disorder and noise.

After their crime, the parents *express some regret* but *remain convinced of the necessity of instilling discipline in all young people from very early on.* Almost always, these parents belong to *small family units that cultivate a certain suspicion toward others and quite a few pretensions.* They are *fixated on themselves and their children,* they have *few friends or interests outside of work and television.* They are *unsociable* and *distrust everything that is not familiar.* They consider *order and cleanliness to be supreme values;* their household is *a stronghold, nothing has the right to undermine it.*

I barely dare to say that these *asocial* American parents, *who are abnormal in the way they exaggerate what's normal and usual to absurdity*—but who, as Doctor Hacker says, *suffer very little from personality disorders:* they *make their children suffer from them*—oddly resemble ordinary French parents. And the familial closed doors of the persecutors on the other side of the Atlantic are in many ways equivalent to those of our peaceful and very private French households.

The killers and those who don't kill are normal from top to bottom: there's nothing special about them, except for the fact that they take order to the letter. Since the criteria for "mental health" is "responsibility"—orthodoxy in behavior, speech, work and morals—psychiatry is incapable of assigning "pathology" to criminality that would be the sufficient and necessary symptom of "disease" if it occurred out of this framework (profession-property-family). Psychiatry has to remain silent at the point where the order that it protects commences; and although it's been tearing "maladjusted" kids submitted to it to shreds for years, it can only offer a certificate of normalcy to adults who are so well adjusted that they murder in order to adjust others.

As proof of that perfect adjustment, according to F. Hacker, this is the pattern of thought in French families—I mean in the families of American persecutors: *all criminal parents consider the family model of their existence to be a natural and eternal institution that represents and expresses moral and traditional values. Blindly and uncritically they transmit the laws in force. Inside themselves,* these parents *have completely and blindly adhered to the schemas and frameworks of society.*

Doctor Hacker thinks that in a great number of cases, this rigidity is due to the fact that the persecutor parents have themselves endured a battered childhood, a very severe and very brutal education. As confirmation of this, it is asserted that mistreated children who don't die *remain attached to their parents despite the pain and disfigurement they've endured.* They even admit *having deserved the punishment; they accept the abuse with fatality, as evidence of affection and interest.*

Even better: these battered children *show signs of a bad conscience, they're persuaded that they are guilty of disobedience and thoughts of rebellion, even though they don't remember them.* And Doctor Hacker concludes: *the feeling of guilt instilled in the child's mind by his father and mother works to rehabilitate and legitimize his parents.*

I don't think I need to add much more. The situation of the battered child, the way parental power is exercised, the oedipal deal of survival it imposes in an authoritarian way, the child's libidinal and emotional investments in the figures of the familial bell jar, are strictly the same, whether it's a matter of the worthy and happy child and his nice worthy parents (*Hachette Encyclopedia*), or the persecuted child, subject to the violence of his "too normal" parents. The child-reward is exploited limitlessly, "discipline" is instilled in him, he is made the privatized object of dad-mom's pleasure—he is purely and simply robbed of his life. If he seems to still be alive or has to be buried, the difference is a completely formal one: inside it's the same.

If I called parental abuse "oedipal," it's primarily because of the age of the victims—less than four. These children are undergoing oedipalization, but in a context in which the castrator deal has no compensation for them. Authoritarian, cold parents, showing very little affection; puritanism and discipline; the child is cut off and receives nothing, and over time begins to appreciate the abuse itself as a kind of emotional and sexual bonus: ultimate adjustment of his desire to the parental sources. Without this adjustment, these deprivations are going to disrupt his behavior: physical disorders, a lack of discipline, capricious appetites, screaming, tears, insomnia, masturbation, all these things provoked by the severity of the parents, who'll increase it more. Those who "wanted" the child find out that he's not what they were told he'd be but is instead a little insolently alive being, abominably organic, infernally corporeal, irregular, selfish, amoral. Such "nature" isn't what they had been taught; so their child is abnormal, monstrous, he has to be straightened out as soon as possible.

They're like every parent who exists: they insert the child into a market they're not conscious of (food and well-being for submission of the body and suppression of sex); only, their rigorous convictions keep them from fulfilling their part of the bargain, since in their eyes the normality of the child is not something that you buy for him over time, but an immediate "natural" element that comes before any possible deal. When you have several kids, the child that you torment, explains Doctor Hacker, is the one you *prefer to his brothers and sisters*; he embodies the values in which you believe more than everything, he is the superego image that you develop of yourself and others: he has to be irreproachable since he represents you.

Such a passionate investment prevents you from having the mixture of patience and indifference toward him that you have toward other children in the family. You forget that it takes six or eight years before a child knows how to refrain from all exterior signs of a corporeal, or "deviant," existence; and you go too far in the job of bringing back the youngest to healthy ideas about the human-being, or, should I say, "human-seeming."

This kind of parental violence is a maximum tensing of the diffuse violence inherent in "normal" adult-child relations. Parents who don't persecute are content with moderate violence, non-excessive mistreatment, invisible psychic abuses and sexual torment that seem affectionate on the surface. This is how they transform the newborn into a boy or girl, a copy that conforms to the child slave that is wanted. Brutal parents, on the other hand, prove to be incapable of putting up with the little one's "deviance," and the child must resemble the correct model right away: every evening, he is coldly retouched with blows of the hammer. If familial education strives to eliminate the child, to associate the new human being's humanity with a capacity for stifling himself, for obeying, for putting up with things, for *conforming blindly and without criticism to the rules in force, for seeing the familial form of his existence as a natural, eternal institution*, then it is quite obvious that education that normalizes the child and that which destroys it are one and the same thing. The implicit axiom of parental power is that there is only one kind of child: a dead child.

If he can stick to the crushing psycho-sexual role assigned to him by the family without a problem, everything will be alright. But if he rebels, if his eyes open, if he *criticizes the rules in force*, violence is immediately permitted: both gentle parents and brutal parents are entirely in agreement about that, and so are educators, psychiatrists, nice moms, and all the decent people who are upset by the sight of a slap but who, in their own way, also persecute children for the slightest irregularity. You're afraid that the child will slip, you're afraid that he'll imitate you wrongly, you're terrorized by the thought that, because of him, or because of you, tomorrow will be different from today—and everything that you consider "natural" and "eternal" will be nothing more than dust in your hands.

For the immense majority of adults, the order that they transmit and that does harm is also the one that keeps them going; and they fear its destruction much more than they suffer from its rule. This is why we keep from interfering when we hear the neighbors straightening out their brats. They know what they're doing, they're working for the common good.

There is a surprising contrast, by the way, between those people who refuse to heed the wails of a kid who is being persecuted by his father and those passersby who "understand immediately" the first call of children who are being bothered by an adult. What a quick response to justice on the one hand, and what hesitation on the other!

No mystery, however: the unknown person on the street is a thief, while the persecutor at home is an owner. It's up to him to manage his property as he sees fit. He can count on others to keep watch over his progeny when its outdoors and to remain noninquisitive when he gets it back safe and sound and gives it a pounding. "And then, parents can't be cruel, only wicked men are, the ones who give others' children the eye. Look at who they are talking about in the papers, they've been talking about it for months: a strangler, they've been showing the photo of the little girl on the news every night, she was so cute, what a monster, what are the police doing about it? But those thousands of children killed by their parents, I don't believe it, that would have to be around twenty-five a day, that's got to be made up: for one thing, you never read about it, and you don't see the faces of the kids on TV, not twenty-five, not one. There's your proof."

Parental crimes are covered up by general consent of the adults protecting the family. It was only in 1971 that the French National Assembly passed a law that in theory opened a breach in the secrecy concerning parental power. On one hand, doctors are absolved from the obligation of professional confidentiality when they observe "abuse or deprivation inflicted upon children of less than 15 years." (Hmm, you stop being a minor awfully fast when it comes to abuse. That would be O.K. if adolescents had the right to have sex at the same age as they have the right to be tortured in peace— or at least the right to leave.)

On the other hand—and within the framework of Article 63 of the penal code, which punishes those who do not come to the assistance of those in danger—"those who are witnesses of the said abuse and deprivation" are expressly required to report them.

One would hope that his would remedy the silence of doctors and the cowardice of neighbors. In practice, this law hasn't had any effect. Doctors have the *right*, according to their code of practice, to report abuse, but they're not obligated to do so and they continue to abstain. Sometimes, even, in the interest of the children: the parents would be afraid of being reported by the doctor and would no longer dare contact him to take care of the victim. As for those famous "neighbors," they don't do any more denouncing than they did before and prefer to risk going to prison—they're mostly afraid that the reported parents will get even and come kick their ass.[16]

To put it briefly, the persecutors make terror reign and keep the situation well in hand. The kindness of the order is taken as a trap for the respect for order. The neighbors let brutal parents act out of fear of being beat up: let that happen to the kids, not to me. And the doctors let the abuse go on so that they'll have a chance to intervene later. Two weird reasons? As soon as it's a question of parental power, everything becomes weird.

---

16. *France-Soir*, September 13, 1972. Here again, what's said confirms the "normality" of the torturers: they seem reassuring, "as expected." These are people like everybody. Like you and me!

The statistics I was citing, for example—or, rather, what's missing from them. There are deaths, serious injuries, but where are the simple acts of violence? Those that lead to less bleeding or that don't disfigure the victim? And what about their frequency? How long each time, how many times a day, how many days a year, how many years during childhood? All of that is a family secret, a secret about property, a secret about the private life, a secret of education, a secret about the rights of the adult, a secret of power. You don't measure it unless it boils over. It's only "with the greatest reticence" that facts like I have cited are divulged, bit by bit. The real mores of the silent majority are still almost empty of any exploration; it's not even scientific to talk about them, impossible to draw from them a sociology with equations; so let's put up with them and kick the bucket since they're not good material for theses. Silent majority? Well protected, rather; well covered up by an enormous conspiracy of silence.

A few conjectures. The family situation that corresponds to the statistics for "filicide" and the abuse that we've managed to record has certain characteristics. Husband 20 to 30, children of an early age. So this is a mediocre privatization of the nuclear family, closed though it may want to be. In a household of the young, the neighbors are less embarrassed about intervening than in one with settled adults; less embarrassed about reporting it, as well. We spy on couples with a baby, whereas we lose interest in flesh-for-coddling if it's aging; they're children without diapers and less grope-worthy. What is more, the little ones make a lot more noise than the others when you hit them, and for a lot longer; it's noticed, it moves us more—and even if it's just some teething, we get worried, lend an ear, interpret it, it gets under our skin. Finally, the very young child who has endured extreme abuse could have problems recovering by himself, you're afraid that he'll end up in your hands—croaking—you'll need a doctor, or the hospital. There are so many reasons for revealing tortures, none of which exist in the years that follow early childhood.

By then, the parents have aged, we respect them. The children have grown, the neighbors are hardly preoccupied with it any longer: a baby was a bit like the common good, the older child is their business. He's reached a state in which he exasperates parents less than the "deviant" life of the very small child appalled them. He doesn't soil himself any more, he gets by, he has some discipline, he goes to school, he no longer has sex organs, he knows how to play the game. He'll no longer stir up any abuse but the institutional kind—punishment for transgressing codes; laziness, lying, being impolite, damaging his clothing, the home, small thefts, prohibited sexuality, irregular kinds of leisure activities, etc. Thus parents have fewer opportunities for killing him. And besides, if they do keep beating as often and as hard, well, the child has become robust, he dies less easily. It's an advantageous kind of strength: no need for a doctor after a session, you can fix him up at the house, no leaks. A few daubs of make-up on some black-and-blue marks, some burns to put ointment on, bandages to hide the rest, or shutting him up for a few days so that he won't be seen too soon at school: he had a "fever." He "fell," he got into a "fight"; this is the age for cuts and bumps, even if they didn't happen as we say. The familial privatization of the child and the abuse is now at a maximum. Heartfelt philanthropy remains at the door, or, rather, only dares open those of the poor, who are meant to be "butchers"—even though they don't beat up any more than people in the middle class do.

Another hypothesis: little by little suicide takes over for parental murders. The deaths will be allocated to other statistics, a kind that will be even more difficult to establish and interpret: this is—par excellence—the domain of the familial secret, of guilt and parents' shame, as if those who died were denouncing more serious abuse than you can do with a poker. Or as if the parents were discovering, to their amazement and incredulity, that exercising even physically nonviolent power over someone, that suppressing, training, normalizing them, can also kill.

Suicide of those 10 to 14 is "only" the *11th cause* of death. It becomes the *3rd cause* from ages 15 to 19. For young adults age 10 to 24, it will be the *second cause*, accidents topping everything in all three cases (and I won't have the bad taste to bring up the problem of the responsibility of or intervention by parents in those accidents, which are the first cause of the mortality of minors of all ages—hyper-family-centricized as France obviously is).

These are successful suicides. Since it's not the amount of corpses that interests me, but the desire to destroy oneself—the ultimate response of the minor to his familial and social destruction—here are the figures for attempts, unsuccessful suicides, by year, for the same ages: 20,000, at least 5,000 of whom are in high school.[17]

There are important points in common between the mortality of those 10–20 and that of the younger children. Vague circumstances,

---

17. Doctor A. Haim, *Les suicides d'adolescents*, Payot 1970. The figure for attempts is very difficult to establish: each time that it is possible, they are hidden or bowdlerized by the "guilty" one's circle.

In addition, we observe two times as many suicides among boys as among girls. Without commentary, since no one knows what a boy or a girl can be. We only know into which kind of truly distinct machine each infant is transformed by society, based on biological sex, and consequently it is probably these artificial psychosocial data that also determine the difference between the dead.

secretiveness of parents, no relationship between the "accident" and the economic or socio-cultural level of the family, a perfectly regular distribution of the phenomenon throughout all social classes, the existence of exterior rules for the adolescent in his first contacts with society that exactly match those that preside at the time of the newborn's first contact with the closed and repressive universe of the family; everything coincides. Same causes, context, effect: you could say that during childhood, it's the parents who kill; after, it's the children who liquidate themselves.

In this case as well, it's not a question of isolating the measurable phenomenon in order to suggest that there is nothing else involved. Just as thousands of the murdered represent only a minority of persecuted children, adolescent suicides, whether successful or not, are only the exceptional borderline cases of a situation that all the others live as well.

Let's recall the effect of abuse on the young child: *he remains attached to his parents*, he thinks he is *guilty of disobedience and thoughts of rebellion*, that *feeling of guilt* is instilled in him forever, he becomes an adult who submits *blindly and without criticism to the rules in force*. Work-family-television. This is the ideal child and the model citizen. And Filium's esteemed authorities, denouncing the universality of physical and mental violence between adults and minors, candidly reveal to us the only way that the order can survive. The visible blunders of the reproduction of the order—traumatized torture victims taken to the hospital, "overly normal" citizens, thousands of children killed, thousands of suicidal adolescents, or those who have committed suicide—every social class and every country coughs them up at the same time. They're the write-offs of exploitation, the irregulars of the slave factory. We're beginning to get statistics about them, to know them, the secret is surfacing slowly. Fathers, Inc.

knows they're guilty, knows that people will realize it, and they are getting ready to change tactics. In this moment of failure, the order is hesitating between authoritarianism and liberalization; unsure of the success, they're playing both sides at the same time, opening a door there, drawing a bolt somewhere else, reflecting, revising, doing the opposite, endeavoring to combine everything in one action.

And "liberalism" in terms of sexual information is exactly that. They hold onto the keys of freedom, they're going to sell them to you, and the lock as a bonus: with all that, buckle up well. Yes, a key closes, and a key opens. They give us one for opening and explain to us which direction to turn it in—watch out, the other direction could be dangerous for you. But the direction that's allowed is the one that closes. It's not about sexual freedom without instructions for suppressing it.

Another question. In such a society is it easy and fun, or difficult and painful to live a life of free love, to refuse to get married or to have sexual ownership of another, the giving-to-get of well-behaved love, procreation, unequal roles, censure, authority? Will you live as peacefully as the fathers of families, or will you endure a daily war? If you choose pleasure outside of the market, if you choose autonomy, the sociability of desire, what will you be: a free and happy person, or a deviant disowned by everyone and followed by the police? According to the doctors: *precocious sexual relations risk steering young people toward a search for pleasure alone. Yet love is born from the encounter between physical pleasure and sentiment. One without the other induces bitterness and disillusionment.*[18]

Science certainly isn't ever at loss to amaze us. Soon it will be telling poorly raised children that using a swear word will lead to

18. *Hachette Encyclopedia*, volume 3 (14–16 years).

paranoia and will *risk steering them* toward the asylum—where you are very *unhappy* and have a lot of *destitution to protest.* Though I must agree with our authors. The *search for pleasure* is reserved for the rich. Others will be put through the mill if they lay a finger on it. We'll rain down on them so much that they'll become *sick. Their sexuality will never reach a normal stage:* they won't have children, and they'll *get even* on ours, instead of killing theirs like everyone else does.

Yes, the only "bitterness" that *physical pleasure* (the medical baseness of the body) devoid of *sentiment* (the medical nobility of the soul) can produce is that of the flawed, the poorly castrated who are hunted down by the order that the *Encyclopedia* teaches.

According to it, happiness is being healthy, sexual health is to be in love; if possible, both of you, and, if possible, for your whole life— on condition, besides, that you are of age, a man and a woman, married, good citizens and eager to have a baby. When it comes to *physical pleasure,* there's neither woman nor man, nor marriage nor golden wedding anniversary, nor age nor country, nor newborn nor revenue; all those things are represented by the indispensable *sentiment.* You can see why pleasure is bad without it.

Since there are babies behind this reasoning yet again, let's talk about them. I think I've demonstrated their purpose for normal people as well as for "overly normal" people. Private ownership of children is society's psycho-sexual compensation for adults, in exchange for their submission to the market of production-exploitation and its *rules in force*—which include the prohibition against pleasure. Sex education aims to uphold that submission, to increase its advantages, to brighten up the prison. It insists more than ever on the role of the baby-reward (completely indispensable to marriage-happiness) in the well-normalized and well-suffocated libidos of the submissive exploited. It binds children and adolescents

to obedience, to chastity, to blind respect and to believing that *the family model of their existence* is *natural and eternal.* It holds out to them the faraway hope of *having* (sinister verb) their own children. It prepares these future parents for inflicting on babies thus obtained the same fate of the child-objects that are being tortured or caressed, twisted, mentally destroyed. And this entire little world will grow up, become like the good adults—antisocial, rigid, frustrated, intolerant, obsessed with privatization, ownership, power. Precisely those adults who police and exploit this society in which pleasure is "illusory and bitter."

Such is the astonishing completion of the loop that our doctors have managed to accomplish—so concerned about sparing us an unhappy life, but teaching only what will make it even worse. Their praise for conjugal pleasure takes on a very different weight when you oppose it to the aggressive line of argument they use to condemn the "spendthrift" pleasures of the minor. Let us admire their wisdom, their clear-headedness, their concern for the common good, their love of the truth, and finally, their understanding of the society in which we live.

Suddenly today's Danes have made up their minds to encourage the tragedy of *precocious physical pleasure*—condemning a healthy youth to *bitterness* and *disillusionment.* The news was announced in France to almost no reaction. However, it's quite significant; but at the moment when the French papers, in the name of sex education, were opening their columns to pew-renters and students' parents so that they could discuss how many angels could screw on the head of a pin, it would have been embarrassing to announce that in Denmark the sexual majority had just been lowered to 14.[19]

---

19. *Le Monde*, February 18-19, 1973. The citations that follow are extracted from this article.

This isn't about the right to marry: the law henceforth in force specifies that Danish boys and girls of 14 *will be able to obtain contraceptives and condoms without the authorization of their parents.* No babies in view, the disillusionment is certain. No ring on your finger, what bitterness!

Since you become incapable of "loving someone else" when you masturbate, and you prefer "physical pleasure" to "love" when you fuck precociously, Danes, who'll have jerked off before the age of 14 and copulated after are going to become the most savage people in Europe. France is already trembling and preparing for battle.

What "unbalanced people" who don't understand "the functioning of their bodies" have voted in such a law in the Danish parliament? Psychologists, sociologists, educators, who were *calling for these measures for years.* Horror of horrors, they have received the support of the *homophile groups who have been fighting energetically against the discriminations in the code of law.* Here we have the correctors of children and those who pervert them in solidarity, the former abandoning the policing of flies that the latter like to open. It's up to adolescents to decide themselves, that's what the law says.

The "unbalanced" have pointed out that *in our times girls and boys are more mature at 14 than adolescents of the same age in preceding generations. Since their sex life has a tendency to begin a lot earlier, why hinder it if it has a real need to develop?*

What kind of malarkey is that? When *the sex life has a tendency to begin,* you definitely shouldn't have sex, come on now, you'll get sick—you need to "reread the book with Dad." And

---

19. *Le Monde,* February 18–19, 1973. The citations that follow are extracted from this article.

doctors have told us over and over again, what really *hinders the sex life* is having one.

So, what's the sense of these simplistic arguments? Who are these adults who for years have "contested the sexual destitution" of adolescence? Their dad never told them anything about that.

Let's have done with it. Reform in Denmark: Danish youth *will cope with it.* They'll be nothing problematic about their sexual autonomy: no repressive education to instill either desire, the body, the sex organs, "deviancies," gratuitous pleasure with guilt. And since families over there are a lot more open than we are, and their children enjoy a greater freedom in their comings and goings, and at an earlier age, the sexual emancipation of the minor won't represent the enormous revolution of mores that it would in our country, in the eyes of parental power. It will be quite unnecessary to assure children that pleasure is better when it's shared; they'll be able to find out for themselves, and to determine alone and at their whim if orgasms at 100% profit are bigger than the 0% masturbatory, or the "minus 100%" perverted ones. They'll have received frank, concrete and practical sex information without lies and without moralizing. They'll know that pills aren't only for popping into deserving mothers' mouths, and condoms not only for the knobs of fathers with six kids; they'll use them to have sex for pleasure, without babies, problems, calculations and shame. What's more, condoms are a gas to jerk off in, and they make nice balloons for little brother. He'll probably go burst them on the sly to get even for not having the right himself to some pleasure.

The girls will have a clitoris. On the other hand, they won't have the duty to have a child, but to avoid it carefully. Equal in pleasure, in freedom, in responsibility, they *won't learn* submission to the male and the obsession for mothering, whereas boys *won't learn* domination and power.

In Denmark, obviously, the "big guys from eighth grade" will be a serious danger for their juniors. They'll know and do too much, and the others not enough. They'll write horrible things on locker doors. There will doubtlessly be hidden feelings of solidarity between the big guys who've reached the age of consent and the little ones who haven't but certainly would like to "develop" even so. And maybe a wave of debauchery will reach all the way down to the grade school children, who knows, to the littlest of all—who, between two sessions of abuse, won't get over having desired something else besides dad and mom.

Reform in France. Boys of 14, informed sexually, will be afraid. They won't know anything about girls, and will know almost nothing about themselves. They'll be afraid of adults and the outside world. They'll be able to masturbate secretly while worrying about diseases of the mind. Fourteen-year-old girls, informed sexually, will be afraid. They won't know anything about boys, and almost nothing about themselves. They'll be afraid of adults and the outside world. They'll be able to masturbate secretly while worrying about diseases of the mind. The girls will be Mothers, and the boys Fathers. And as they wait, at night, at home with their family, each on his or her side, will be thinking about Love.

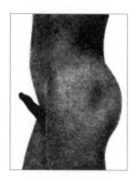 # THE SEXUAL MARKET AND ADOLESCENCE

During the first anxieties about puberty, the adolescent will turn to his mother.[20]

I HAVE ONLY A FEW MORE THEMES to examine in this last chapter, and I will center them around the final period of training for the reproduction of the order: the period during which castrated children learn to one day become castrating parents. Adolescence, in other words.

In the relationship between the minor's family-centric, pubescent and semi-privatized body and the repressive elements of the sexual market, the normalization of the exploited will be developed.

Since we in our country fear any "deviant" imperfection in the finish of the human product, this essential phase can't be left to the random nature of Danish freedoms; and the Hachette volume intended for French adolescents, who are prohibited from having sex, is therefore a veritable catechism of self-repression.

---

20. *Hachette Encyclopedia*, vol. 14–16 years, caption for a photograph.

It's important to differentiate the phases of indoctrination. From early childhood to puberty, the minor is taught orthodox management of his body by castration, parental collectivization, censure, detention, complete build-up of capital. The result is a little subject that is good at management, impatient to invest, well informed about the socio-cultural criteria that allow him to estimate the value of others and his own value. A life outside the family reduced to a minimum strengthens this internalization of values and whets the appetite for ownership, the desire for superiority and power. He or she is "outside" just enough to put this into practice, to refine that indoctrination and load it with images, without risking compromising it by precocious experiences or deviations from management that are too disturbing. We have, finally, a sex-object that is indecipherable and taboo and the future key to the orgasm-ownership machines.

After puberty, these elements remain. Even if you have the right to a sex life, it hardly risks altering the construction of the adolescent as his own property, maintaining marketable, hierarchical relationships with others, conforming to prior roles and the laws of profit. The only possible deviancies will be infrequent and restrained; they will continue to conform to this corporeal and sexual capitalism. They will merely be discredited, "negative" investments, which will be in tune with the values of the desirable—a cultural determinant of which the young child is unaware—and the conventional rituals of pleasure—another cultural element with which you only come to terms after having subjected all desire to it.

In brief, whether he's free or enslaved, heterosexual-conjugal or a cruiser, someone who beats off or a queer, the adolescent makes his appearance on the market like a normal product, meaning that his body, in every case, obeys the social laws of the privatization of the individual and restrictive investments. Whether he buys his partner by amorous giving-to-get (the only form of affective relations that he's been taught) or squanders his desire as so much capital, he'll continue to believe in the trilogy of work-ownership-power and in the social and sexual roles that it controls. He'll remain sheltered from the "danger"—which would be discovering the gratuitousness, freedom, plurality of desire and the *sociability of the body*; or rather, discovering it again, since the child is and lives all of that before the family crushes it.

This freedom, accorded to *finished* machines, is therefore not incompatible with the prosperity of the system; and this is why Danish democratic capitalism has just emancipated minors (Sweden is about to do the same). Only in societies of hyperrepression and crazed exploitation can one see in the minor's "programmed" sexual expenditures a risk for anarchy, dissidence and flight.

So, none of that in our country. What I will quote from the propaganda written for the 14-16 age group will make this obvious.

It seems to me that this double set of numerals, 14-16 years, is enough to indicate the antisexual orientation of the book. In fact, if it was conceivable—not considering censorship—to write books for children that are adapted to their vocabulary, such an educational necessity no longer in the slightest justifies dividing up information for the minor into three minutely differentiated parts responsible for covering the period of sexual frustration from puberty to the legal age of majority: 14-16, 17-18, adults.

But let's start with the last and go backwards. The volume for adults is thick, cultivated, costly, quite up to date when it comes to official sexology. It is illustrated with medical documents, photos of every type (including some female nudes/objects and frightful dads with beards and body hair that you also find in the other volumes: virility of the signs of power covering the body of the Master, femininity as an exhibtion of surfaces to conquer). There are also works of art, reproductions of paintings, sculptures, prints, which mark out the correct part of the cultural patrimony dedicated to Eroticism in the sexuality of the middle class adult (a noble art/discourse of pleasure, opposed to vulgar, acultural, proletarian and persecuted non-art, which is pornography).

All of it is a reproduction of the already commercialized sexology of France, modernized here as merchandise by a well-put-together edition: let's not forget that this book is expensive, and the targeted customers are privileged parents from the middle classes.

The information, which is neither new nor more objective than the others, overhauls its look by a penchant for the topical, "journalistic" aspects—in the *Paris-Match* sense of the word.

In the volume for adults, as well as in the ones for ages 17–18 and 14–16, they have avoided the pitfall of pornography, obscentity, the outrageous: no photographs of erections—they don't even reproduce the document, unique to France, in the volume for ages 10–13—no photograph of a vulva (there are some nice explicit diagrams), no intercourse shown at the angle where there's something to see, medically speaking. It isn't censorship, obviously, it isn't cowardice about the frankness that the medical "cover" of the works was permitting; it's simply that such photos are superfluous. Adults don't need them any more, whereas children or adolescents would be unpleasantly traumatized by them—or, even worse, incited to that *physical pleasure* that you *share* with a piece of printed paper, when you have nothing else. Pleasure that evokes that of starving people chewing the leather of their shoes.

The illustrations make up for it with very slimy images of childbirth in close-up, the babies all wrinkled in incubators and the X-rays of well-filled uteruses.

There's not a cartilage missing in the diagrams of impregnating coitus. The color cross-sections of erections are dynamic enough to wake you up at night. There are all the tiny beasts you could want in the microscopic images of jism.

The strongest accent is on the adaptation of the adult to society and its norms, the only surety for happiness. They bask in a few reflections on sexual equality, the taboos that are disappearing, the right to pleasure within marriage. They sternly remind us of the importance of men and women submitting to the father-role and mother-role, upon which depends the future normality of their own children, that is to say, their ability to play these roles exclusively and rigorously when the time comes.

The volume for ages 17-18 is identical to all that, but less cultivated. Less Freud, less philosophical reflection, a negligible amount of "artistic" illustration, much more inflexible warnings, but in a reasonable, moderate tone; they're talking to the "big teenagers." The content of the book, however, is less like the volume for adults than the tissue of nimble lies and "managed" medical information that we saw in 10–13 years and that dominates, even more dispassionately, 14-16 years.

A strange kind of composure. Because these books insistently take the risk of being subjected to the critical minds of students— but the propaganda couldn't give a fig about being detected, this isn't its concern. It already knows that it won't convince any of its rebellious readers, young as they are; it won't reform any of the teenagers getting a good laugh out of its pro-birth and antisex gobbledygook; it won't convince a single happy meat-beater to give up his pleasures, nor one homosexual kid to daydream about the opposite sex, and so on. What it wants to do is to reign over the vast universe of feeble brains that has been well prepared, well twisted by the family and school; to regiment the sexualities that are a bit off, all the impressionable ones, the timorous, all the frustrated ones consumed by shame rather than revolt—all the resigned ones from the two sexes. Those who passively put up with the family, school-work, the nasty Outside, and who won't hesitate to hand over their sex to the educator so that he can redo it for them.[21]

It should be kept in mind, regarding all of this, that we're dealing with objective sex information, sincerely drafted by some scrupulous doctors who want to be useful to their fellow man. They're upset that there are still so many prohibitions, so much guilt, fear and obstacles to happiness; they are sorry that we have distrusted pleasure for so long, and that for so long we have exploited the inferiority of women—and done it despite the fact that they can become Mothers! It is only in small places between the lines of their explanations that we can flush out all these blights that they're fighting so fiercely and transmitting so well. The Order no longer resides in clauses of the code of law: it invisibly saturates every sentence of the "liberal" discourse. The authors need a nice big subject that is really at odds with procreative ideology in order to bare teeth uncovered by a smile.

---

21. These reflexes of obedience are due only to an acquired docility, and we can guess how: they are exactly those of the battered child. Whether mentally or physically doesn't matter; the result is the same, and it happens to the majority of kids in families.

The work for ages 14-16, which I will quote as needed to wrap things up, is a maximum reduction of the learned and well-organized material in the volumes for those who are older. It is composed of questions and answers, like all catechisms and all propaganda brochures.[22] These questions *are real ones asked by teenagers* during *educational talks* given by the authors. Rather "biased" information if we are to believe the import of the questions that the speakers in these talks managed to dig out of their audience.

In them, there is little theorizing, practically no pondering, they "guide" and force you into things with alacrity. Openly repressive information represents 44 pages—consecrated to the "psychology" of puberty and adolescence. Medical information, insidiously working to cause guilt and jam-packed with bogeymen takes up 95 pages. No more "art" at all in the illustrations (the readers are too young to understand the representations of middle class Eroticism, overseen by the male heads of the family and their luxury bookshops). Coitus has been reduced to the essentials with well-done sketches in color pencil: these cocks in cross-section are already so obscene that they have to be surrounded with the cross-section of a vagina to show where the little wrigglies go to find the big egg.

There's no more story, a family romance like those in the volumes for the younger children. They speak directly to the minor, like elder brothers, like human beings plain and simple, who help and loyally advise. A loyalty I am about to assess.

Disappearance of the family. This, for example, is the only father/son interaction in the work:

---

22. The passages in italics that follow are taken from the volume commented upon.

How did the young and athletic dad for ages 10–13 suddenly become this fat jerk shown only up to the nape of his neck, with his big ass and suspenders, the detestable image of Power? And why has good decorating and the lovely second home given way to this seedy place?

One thing is sure: you can't hope to seduce the reader any more by scenes of family bliss. He's going through a period of dissidence, revolt, painful frustration; to shove a family under his nose would be an enormous blunder. You don't talk about rope in the house of a hanged person.

And thus, this vindictive photo (impeccable doublet of the man-in-the-park for ages 10–13), meant to rub the teenager the right way: *This book was written for you by two men and two women, all four of whom are doctors… We hope that it will show you the way to a better understanding of the things of life.*[23]

All the iconography yields to the necessity of rubbing out the tyrants and showing hope—the fictitious kind. So much so that its antifamily stance corresponds to the same emotional and effective touting as the family photos of the preceding volume.

Family: 6 photos; babies: 3 photos. Outside world: 35 photos.

In them you see groups of adolescents, boys and girls together or looking into each other's eyes, hand-kissing (but of course). Posters, demonstrations, Women's Lib, streets, cars, motorcycles, movie theaters, the urban landscape, all the "permissive" stuff. The outside world has finally been authorized: no more sadist behind every tree; instead, future spouses on every public bench. How the world has changed, suddenly! The proof:

---

23. Preface *For Teenagers* at the beginning of the volume. This whorish foreword is followed by another that (behind the young reader's back—with stunning bad manners, since he can read it, too) is intended *for parents*. It is explained to them—while dealing carefully with their oversensitivity as owners and their touchy morality—who the adolescent is: an unhappy, anxious, sexually obsessed, wretched rebel whom they just had to address in a familiar, informal way. For several virtuous reasons, they go on to say, he must be granted "complete sexual information" (sic)—*it's better that there be no censorship at all,* the authors declare courageously. No, the adolescent must be faced head on, gently, you should play it with tolerance, invite him to pour out his "problems," cleanse him of his disturbances, because *he must achieve a certain identification of the image that he has of himself with the parental images.* Something that the violent parent/child relationship endangers and that the good educator will know how to manufacture: *all dialogue has a therapeutic virtue.*

One will appreciate the quality of the "dialogue," the elegance of the technique—and the incredible crudeness of the avowal.

Depictions of sex organs (photos devoted to "external genital organs"):

        —children: boy, 0; girl, 0.

        —teenagers: boy, 0; girl, 0.

        —adults: man, 0; woman, 0.

Depictions of the naked body (photos):

        —children: boy, 1; girl, 0.

        —teenagers: boy, 2 (anthropometric, back/front, headless, cock reduced to jelly); girl, 2 (the same, genitals invisible).

        —adults: man, 1 (it's the one with the beard); woman, 4 (properly anthropometric, 3. "Artistically" naked, 1).

Reproduction: 28 photos, 44 drawings.

Contraception: 6 photos, 6 drawings.

Erotic Activity: (images devoted to some practice of pleasure): 0.

Not true: out of the kindness of my heart, I'm going to classify here the *only* photo of (hetero-procreative) intercourse. It's a naked man lying on top of a naked woman and, since the women is hiding the head of the man with her head, which the arm of the man is hiding, you can't see their filthy, disgusted faces. You don't see the rest of it, either, because the photo is cut off… at the waist.

Yes, the world of age 14–16 certainly has changed. The family isn't a source of pleasure? We're hiding that. The outside makes you drool with envy? Look, here it is.

It's like an inversion of the life of the adolescent. Showing some frustrated types these images of freedom, this welcoming outside, without cops, prohibitions, sexual misery, is like photographing a few prisoners on the promenade, washed, decked out and wearing blush to prove to world opinion that people are well treated in concentration camps. I'm exaggerating? I'm having a hard time forgetting certain statistics I cited earlier. From ages 15 to 19, suicide is the third highest cause of mortality. Attempts at it, nonmeasurable. Those thousands of annual deaths, those thousands of near-suicides reclaimed and covered up by the family: does this really evoke hand-kissing, smiles, streets where you meet and talk, a life full of hope and the right to exist?

And the situations themselves that are photographed, what's going on in them? Is this really "happiness," or just a few nice little traps for idiots, orgasm-prisons that impose ten laws in exchange for one permission? Is the adolescent's withdrawal from society a lack of nerve or one last hesitation before the labyrinth of codes that are going to cut his desire into pieces the moment that he wants to live it?

The family may be absent, but it reigns over the reader—as testified by the tactless address to the parents. A new double game has to be inaugurated. *Let's initiate a dialogue.*

In all the languages of power, that sentence means: time to lure the prey. Let's inform: because *it makes it possible—if not to resolve problems—at least to tackle what they are.* In fact, you're tackling problems less than you're tackling who has them—rebels who will have to deal with the police-like barricades of "complete sex information."

These *difficulties of adjustment,* this *confusion that an immense majority of young people share,* let's face it frankly, let's answer the questions posed by adolescence. The first one in the book: *What's a baby look like at the very beginning of its life, in the belly of its mother?*

Like the parents in volume 10–13 years, the authors' *eyelashes have fluttered imperceptibly*—but here it comes, they're willing to describe the primordial Egg, with *that indispensable knowledge of the problems of teenagers that they've gone to the source to find.*[24]

---

24. From the preface *For Teenagers.*

Does this seem grotesque? There is, however, a direct relation-ship between the reader's confusion and the baby in the answers, because the baby is the answer. And, in order to validate it, all information has to be organized around it. First the girl and boy will have to acquire the feeling of the legitimate purpose of the "sex organs," which produce what's needed to make the egg; and *there are also external sex organs.* They will be explained the physiology of emissions and ovulation, diseases, periods, the biology of sexual relations, instructions for the way to have them, which can only be used by adults, the *couple-and-maternity*, contraception, pregnancy. They'll be told what to do while waiting to have the right to these wonders (this is where the "psychological" part of the book starts); the real reasons for this prohibition will be confided to them; they'll be threatened with misfortune if they don't yield to it; the big-brothering session ends with a holocaust of deviants; and cur-tain down. *Once the book has been closed,* conclude the authors, *the adolescent will be directly and personally confronted with the thousand problems that he'll have to resolve and surmount. These are the indis-pensable first steps that this work wished to encourage.*

This invariable formula for sex education manuals is not the result of a twisted imagination. It is, in fact, in perfect keeping with all writings about sexology meant for adults: which is to say that it conforms to the medicalized methodology that "researchers" apply to the description of sexuality. Such a description moves necessari-ly from the inside toward the outside—from the inner organs to sexual prohibitions, from "the egg" to life in society. In this way, the basis of the Order is asserted biologically. This is, unfortunate-ly, the exact opposite of the organization of events: the sex life of every human being begins with the prohibited and ends with the baby. Consequently, the dangers that threaten the prohibitions also threaten reproduction and the socio-familial order organized around it. It does not seem to be the fact that, on a planet with three billion inhabitants, the fate of the "species" (and species it is) would be compromised if humanity reproduced a lot less; so when a prohibition gives way, what we fear is not a decrease in the production of babies, which can easily be produced, but the simple fact that the reproduction of the exploiting social order is less certain. Bodies no longer obliged to procreate deprivatize, move away from the family-centric mode, liberalize the social roles of Man and Woman, break through the barriers of power and property that transformed each human for each human into an infinitely distanced Other, finally spurn the system of production/consumption that was exploiting the lacks that they now no longer feel. In short, at the far end of sexual freedom, civilization begins, and the society of exploitation dies.

Not only is this not a utopian perspective, but it's the conscious, nagging fear experienced today by all the guardians of power. And among other things, it is what inspires them to begin reinforcing the existing order by means of liberalist propaganda. "Pleasure," currently so in fashion, will always be able to be bought by the rich, and little by little this new and very old sector of "services" will be liberalized and structured: brothels (pardon me, "eros centers"); written, photographed, filmed pornography; "erotic" art; sex tourism offering fresh or exotic flesh; vacations organized around fucking; commerce in the-more-wicked-the-more-expensive "perversion," commerce in extra-marital hookups (personals or private encounters at weekend hotels), etc.—so many things that are only in the cottage-industry phase, and which, no longer reserved only for the upper middle classes, will attract customers from the middle classes in general. This will only be a supplementary profit system, based on the frustration that conditions them all. An opportunity, as well, for social promotion: the pretty girls and pretty boys born of low station will negotiate their small amount of capital here, and the demand will be so enormous that there will be room for everyone. As for those frustrated ones who are unmarketable and have no cash, they'll only be able to envy these consumers from afar, to be zealous about "succeeding"; and to make up for it, finally, with the consummation of a family and children. This will calm them and keep in place for one more generation those prosperities enjoyed by the dominant class.

The medicalization of sex information coincides precisely with that order, which prepares the ground for business, for resignation and for greed. It legitimizes frustrations that create "demand" and consolidates the restrictions that will endow sexual products with value. It teaches that pleasure for free is impossible; society will teach that all pleasures are to be sold. You will have the right to sexualities of expenditure if you first spend to buy them.

The occupation of the body by repression entails two undisputed laws: woman's duty is to be penetrated, men's is not to be. For him, confiscation of his anus; and for her, description of her body as a place of "conquest," the sole thrill of which comes from invasion: cocks open it and babies bloat it. Adaptation of the organ into an inferior-feminine abyss for the organ as a superior-masculine plenum; inner organs as a deep starting point for a path of penetration/impregnation that moves toward the outside.

Let's go back to the text a bit—I will, of course, respect the strict order of the questions and chapters. *What do the ovaries look like? The Fallopian tubes? The sac that holds the child?* What is the vagina made of? Medical answer: *the vagina comes after the uterus.* First it's connected to the "baby sac," and only then to the outside world.

This is the vulva. And the clitoris, *which is very sensitive* to contact *during sexual relations*. But the exterior of those relations is the devil, for the adolescent; and the authors, under pretext of calming fears, are more than happy to draw up a list of them: two pages on the hymen and the dangers of losing it, concluding—it is time—with a sentence in which you can very vaguely deduct that when it comes to virginity the hymen isn't important. *Can you become a virgin again? Do you lose your virginity the first time you have relations? What is artificial defloration? Can certain sports lead to rupturing your hymen?* (answer: certain sports are *blamed* for it, but these *accidents* are extremely infrequent.) *Can a man always tell that a girl isn't a virgin any more?* There are hymens with small holes and hymens with big holes, so some "men" *wrongly* believe *that a girl isn't a virgin; this is an indication of how little value should be attributed to physical virginity...* Yes, that vague little sentence actually does have a very clear meaning: the only sure merit is virginity that is not only *physical*. It doesn't trick you when you put your finger on it and you know what you're buying.

Now that we know the function and the organ, let's keep "going out of" the body. We have to live with it, which isn't easy: *What's metritis? Salpingitis? Does the vagina get irritated the first time you have relations? What's an ovarian cyst? A fibroid? Aren't there diseases that are considered a disgrace?*

Isn't this information unnecessary for girls and boys who are excessively healthy, albeit virgins? No, because they must follow the revelation of the great mysteries in the ideal order: *gonorrhea* page 40, and *should you remain a virgin?* page 152. First learn what's good (reproduction) and what's scary (diseases). And now, let's talk about the pleasures of being a parent.

But wait, first eleven pages on periods, their periods and their misfortunes—last station of the cross. If they are painful, tell yourself in no uncertain terms that they have to be taken care of, there are effective medicines, *when they're serious enough to have an impact on work every month.*

And here comes Sexual Relations. Yes, I know, it's only Dad and Mom shown from the chest up, and that *instinct that pushes a man and woman toward each other*—pushing them so expertly that they always fall in the same order, Dad on top of Mom.[25] The

---

25. Some data on conjugal mores in France (The Simon Report, 1970). Minimum age of the interviewees: 20.

Positions practiced by the couples: 11% seated, 13% standing, 20% dad on mom's buttocks (but not inside them), 55% mom on dad's tummy-tum-tum. 98% dad on top of mom. Apparently mom-on-top-of-dad is quite widespread; but adolescents mustn't "identify" with that upside-down "parental image," so not a word is said about it. We'll see when the basis for good roles will be firmly asserted (98%), after marriage. That is when the book will tell you everything.

The privatization of coitus: only 10% of the men claim to have had sex "in the presence of a third"; 4% have done it "often." But only 1% of the women have done it. Does this indicate that threesomes are done 90% of the time with whores, or that it happens among men?...

Do they have sex a lot? All the sexologists will answer that it's the quality that counts, and not the quantity—since it's obvious that the less you do it, the better you know how to do it. Statistics: 57% of the interviewees had sex during the month before the study. These 57% are composed of: 17% who screwed 1 to 4 times, 20% 5 to 14 times, 10% 15 to 25 times. This also means that 60% of French people only had sex 0 to 4 times during that month. They have to have done it too much the month before. In any case, we are told that French people 20 to 30 years old, living in cities and not going to church, fuck more than the others.

question that provokes this disclosure about "sexual relations": *how do you make a child?*

Then the text takes an interest in additional phenomena. Can you screw for pleasure? A bad question, too direct: it doesn't allow for a hypocritical answer, and even "yes-but" would seem too extreme. You've got to word it: *are sexual relations only for reproduction?* That way there's still a chance of making the selfish mind of the teenager open to seeing conjugal life as a paradise; and the answer is: *no, sexual relations are not only for reproduction.* Well, can they be for nothing? Come on, let's not get off track: *it's true that man and women form a union not only for the purpose of having a child, but*—man-and-woman? not only? but?—*added to that notion of reproduction*—added?—*is the notion of pleasure. Without seeking to give the other pleasure, there can be no deep satisfaction in it.* So, if you're making a child, you add an effort to it to prevent either partner from grinding his teeth? At least it's clear.

But how do you seek to give *the other pleasure*—with binoculars? With a pendulum? A detective? Put an ad in the paper offering

---

How do they have sex? It happens that 59% of the couples masturbate together, 58% indulge in sucking (but only 8% come that way "frequently"). 19% of the men say they've fucked women in the ass; 14% of the women admit to having been.

The most interesting. During their lives, on average, the men have 12 partners, the women 2. (The exact statistics are 11.8 and 1.8; I'm rounding them off.) 46% of the women have only been intimate with one man; 2% have been intimate with 6 to 14 of them. As for males, 16% have had more than 15 partners in their lives.

5% of the men and 2% of the women have said they have had homosexual relations in their life; 11% of the men and 17% of the women refused to answer. In the U.S.A., 37% of the men and 13% of the women answered yes (Kinsey Report for the period 1930–1950).

a reward to anybody who'll bring pleasure to my wife? And can't he get the pleasure himself, this *other*? Is there something keeping him from it? Or someone? Yes? Why?

There can be no sexual relations without the penis being intro-duced into the vagina. The theoretical, puritanical/pro-birth sex act becomes the focal point of sexual relations, just as "the egg" was for the organs. The questions are going to delineate the objections to this restrictive ritual, the responses will justify its pattern, immor-talize it by ossifying the roles, fears, inequalities and failures that are the result of it, in order, finally, to make them part of the Nature-of-Men and the Nature-of-Women.

Passages from the orgasm-prison:

For a woman, sexual foreplay can be a source of pleasure that is superior to the pleasure of the act itself.[27]

For her, *the start of relations often entails a feeling of guilt. The fear of pregnancy can lead to a distressing sense of inhibition as well.*

Surveys have *always shown that female orgasm was more difficult to achieve than that of males, as if women needed to surmount a host of inhibitions before achieving the full development of their sexuality.*

A lot of feminine frigidity is connected to shortcomings or clumsi-ness on the part of her partner... when a couple sees a doctor, each case must be considered separately.

(Heavy petting, nonpenetrative sexual relations, *the penis remaining in contact with the vulva without pushing through the*

---

27. The Simon Report: 56% of the men and women state that the amount of time they devote to "foreplay" is satisfactory (0 to 9 minutes: 43%, 10 to 14 minutes: 21%, 15 to 45 minutes: 23%).

31% of the interviewees find "foreplay" insufficient, and the majority of these dissatisfied people are... men.

hymen—this type of relations) *leads to a state of tension due to the dissatisfaction of the two partners. The boy must understand that the girl doesn't have the same reasons as he does to give in, and that she may fear an unwanted pregnancy.*

Can sexual relations be painful? In general, no. But losing one's virginity can be.

Impotence for boys: *it's the impossibility of having an erection— an impossibility connected to not enough desire or too much desire: in such cases, it will pass. Feelings of love that are too strong can paralyze a young boy.*

When you're in danger of being "paralyzed," you're a "young boy," and when you "can tell that a girl isn't a virgin any more," you're a "man." These are girls who, when they screw, "prefer" chaste caresses to coitus, whether its reserved and frustrating or "complete" but damaging to the-hymen-that-isn't-important or would risk a pregnancy. Then what causes the "feelings of love that are too strong" that lead, it seems, to male virgins losing their hard-ons, that "too much desire" that produces *premature ejaculations,* which must be associated with impotence, the pain of deflowering, the clumsiness of your partner, *the inhibitions that involuntarily contract the vagina to prevent the penetration of the peni*s, and those that slow down to such an extent *the development of a woman's sexuality*? A mystery. The remedy for all that? A mystery. Oh, there is one: let frustration demolish your brain and your sex organs, and when you've brought your infirmities together within the legitimacy of marriage, go *see a doctor.*

So much for the *pleasure* that is *added* to *reproduction.* Now that we've come to the end of this chapter full of laughs, let's get back to serious things: *the couple and motherhood.* Bizarrely, the chapter with this title, which begins with a full-page photo of mom-baby, is devoted to contraception. We'll soon discover that it's not as contradictory as it seems.

The best method of contraception? *The pill, unquestionably.* How do you get it? *A general practitioner, or preferably, a specialist,* distributes it. Do they really give that to 14-16-year-olds? *According to law, minors younger than 21 will need written permission from one of their two parents.* But that's disgusting! *No, because that law hasn't been applied yet, and for the time being, there are no legal restrictions to prescribing contraceptives for any age.* Translation, which minors know so well: the only restrictions are moral ones that the doctor can apply if he feels like it. The-story-of-the-pill is repeated everywhere: the right-thinking middle class doctor might say yes to middle class girls if they're between 18 and 20 and if he knows the family; unfamiliar patients will have a lot less of a chance; he'll laugh in the face of minors aged 14 and 16—before holding forth with a moralistic speech. Those kids swallow pills that have been pinched and that aren't right for them, this makes them sick, and the job is done. When girls lack those "women's inhibitions," we know how to make them come back.

What about other methods of contraception? *The temperature method?* Complicated, *with a failure rate of at least 10%.* The Ogino method? *No good.* No "guffawing" this time? Coitus interruptus: *failure rate of 25% to 30%. It requires an effort of the will that is especially difficult at the moment of orgasm*—but its *most serious* drawback *is its ineffectiveness.* On the other hand, *there are no mental repercussions for men or women, provided that it doesn't make them feel frustrated.* The best kind of tautology: there are no mental drawbacks to this method, the proof being that there is no drawback—on condition that there is no drawback.

Condoms: a *very effective* method, but *does it entail any mental disturbance?* No, *except if using it results in a feeling of being unfulfilled.*

And does it? *Everything depends upon the individual and circumstances.* But in general, is it disturbing, frustrating, or not? No answer, since the question isn't asked. A well-maintained pattern of information: is it black? No, it isn't black, except when it's black. When is it black? That depends on its color. End of the "dialogue."

Condoms can *be easily bought in pharmacies.* They protect against *venereal diseases.* They can be used *without danger while waiting to employ a more appealing method. Is their use advised during sexual relations for the first time?—It's better to choose a method that is in no way bothersome for the two partners—the pill, in particular.* Oh, so in the end condoms that can be easily bought by minors are *bothersome?* And the pill is *preferable,* that prohibited pill that they give you by prescription when they do give it to you unless they don't give it to you or until the law prevents their giving it to you unless your parents O.K. it ? If I know how to read, the good advice being proffered by the authors is saying: rather than be bothered by a condom while having sex today, don't have sex until you're old enough to *employ a more appealing method.*

The female forms of contraception *the most used? Diaphragms. Can you use them during sexual relations for the first time? No, because usually* the-hymen-that-isn't-important *isn't flexible enough to allow the introduction of a diaphragm.*

Besides, its use *requires some training and an active contribution on the part of the woman,* because you have to put in the diaphragm before fucking and *take it out 8 hours after.*

An *IUD* is much better, *if it is tolerated.* It has to be put in by a doctor, its stays there *permanently and requires no cooperaton on the part of the woman.* Why is it the doctor who puts it in? Because, in the uterine cavity, *strict laws of asepsis must be observed,* if not *you risk getting severe infections.* And there is still, in the end, a *2% risk of failure.*

After this cheery and succinct survey of the allowed but ineffective or bothersome methods and the methods that are effective but furnished only by a doctor, we come back to the pill. If you do take it, how do you avoid *getting fat? The risk is a lot less* today. Does it make you *nervous? Sometimes,* because it *aggravates preexisting conditions.* Do you get *nauseous?* No, *it passes.* Any other dangers? Lets recall those *small drawbacks,* which end when you stop using the pill: *nausea, weight gain, nervousness, to which must be added changes in pigmentation, hair loss, the occurrence of abnormal loss of blood or a lack of bleeding.* Let's enumerate *the dangers that can result because of after-effects: eventual dangers for the children* that you'll have, though this hasn't been proved. *Vascular problems,* yes, admittedly, but that depends on the product. Risk of cancer? It doesn't seem to be increased by the pill. Risk of *sterility?* No, of course not. The chapter ends with a discussion of the pill for men (no, not for a long time, it's complicated medically, and psychologically, *too many men still confuse their virility with their fertility),*[27] irreversible sterilization, legal therapeutic abortion, male and female sterility due to malformations. It will cite a few countries in which abortion is legal.

This, then, is how the libertarian world of pleasures-without-babies is described. Though you may search in vain for a line fit for helping that legendary "full development of a woman" about which the authors—as long as it's not about the full development of a

---

27. A "confusion" the *Encyclopedia* will not spread, as indicated by several questions dealt with: Can a boy be a father before puberty? At what age should you have an operation to preserve normal testicular function if the balls don't descend into their sac? How many spermatozoa do you need to have in your sperm for fertilization to be possible? Not to mention drawings and their ovule-sprinkling erections.

minor—nobly pretend to care, you will, however, find 26 pages devoted to preparing in the minds of girls the full development of the Mother: the long chapter minutely studying *pregnancy*.

A beautiful pregnant blond, full page, naked, in color; then text and images on fertilization, the egg, the embryo, the fetus, pregnancy, delivery, cesareans, premature births, nursing, the baby. In this case, finally, the information is detailed, carefully thought out, calm, soothing; we no longer hear talk about a "danger" in order to say that it doesn't exist but that it exists even so; and if this work reminds us that deflowering hurts, here there are gentle explanations of painless childbirth.

This untroubled chapter completes and crowns the "physiological" part of the work. We've gotten our fill of knowledge about the body, there is now nothing we don't know about mothers and fathers, we've heard about the organs through descriptions of their diseases, about "first relations" through their setbacks, about contraception through its problems and about motherhood through its pleasures. All that remains is to distort desire, caricaturize childhood, make adolescence seem ridiculous and spread fear one last time. The mission of "psychology."

We must tell the minor about his family and sexual history, his past, his present, his situations, by showing "causalities" in order to conceal the repression. References to Freud will help a great deal. The goal, which is never lost sight of for an instant, is for the reader to be persuaded at the very end of the book that *precocious sexual relations risk channeling the young toward a mere search for embittered and illusory pleasure,* and that *sexual relations reduced purely to physical pleasure are dissatisfying* (p. 152).

In the preceding chapter, I commented upon these sterling principles. We observed—and will continue to see—how the authors, joining action to words, composed all their work in such a way that even adolescents not sharing this philosophy are at least endowed with the healthy fears and the doctored ignorance of hazy learning to keep them virtuous.

The psychological account conforms to the usual principle of inversion. It describes the internalizations of Order practiced by the child as if they were natural stages in his development; the repressive, socio-familial cultural elements are not a system of pressures that ought to have explained these stages, but only an interesting setting in which each child develops, the place of an exchange and not an incarceration. The legitimate medical discourse universalizes and eternalizes these actions of the social order.

Passages from forbidden-for-your-own-good:

AT WHAT AGE DO YOU BEGIN TO HAVE SEXUAL NEEDS? *An inattentive observer might believe that the ten-year-old child hardly shows any curiosity for sexual matters… This is because he has had to apply all his energy to the first steps of going to school. However, during that difficult period, sexuality may be in a lull but it certainly exists. Some mornings the boy wakes up with an erect penis. The phenomenon is completely normal.*

MUST YOU DEVOTE ALL YOUR TIME TO WORK? *No, there is a time for play and a time for work… Play, which develops curiosity, imagination and intelligence, is also good schooling for discipline and sociability.*

WHY AREN'T MEN LIKE WOMEN? *Their sex organs are dissimilar, although complementary, and contribute to the same function, reproduction, the birth of a baby. Family and society require different behavior from boys and girls. A boy is naturally aggressive, stronger, more forward and bolder, he's better at math. A girl is softer, more patient, she devotes herself to working with her hands (decorating, cooking), she exhibits thoughtfulness and consistency.*

The boy models his attitude and his behavior on the heroes of the latest western, the little girl on the gentle and timid heroine of a soap opera.

The father and mother represent the entire universe for the child. Toward them he or she feels love mixed with jealousy, demanding complete possession of dad or mom, depending on whether the child is a girl or boy. Thus, learning about affection begins with the parent of the opposite sex.

Encounters between girls and boys, which continue to increase, allow each to become more familiar with the opposite sex, but also to differentiate from them. Until the age of 10, the two sexes were in close contact, teased each other, stopped talking to one another, despised each other, made up, but their games are very different; the boys take refuge in marbles, fighting, boxing or football; the girls prefer dancing, sewing, hopscotch or knitting.

Even in co-ed schools, boys and girls learn in this way to distinguish between masculine and feminine roles. These roles are different but of equal importance, neither can claim superiority over the other.

WHY ARE WE SO INTERESTED IN SEXUALITY AT 15 AND SO LITTLE INTERESTED IN IT AT 10? *The child of 10 is rich in experience, he lives a balanced life in the environment of his family, where the parents serve as exceptional models, and in the environment of school, where he learns essential tasks: he disassociates himself from sexual elements in order to complete his physical, intellectual and social development; in order to become a civilized being, Freud would say, you must pass through such a phase of sexual lull and latency.*

Puberty signals the awakening of the instinct.

IS IT ONLY THE BODY THAT CHANGES DURING PUBERTY? *No, the body is not the only beneficiary of this transformation. Intelligence* undergoes, at the same time as the sex instinct, new development. The adolescent's relations with those around him also change a lot.

IN CASES OF PREMATURE PUBERTY, *the changes arrive 2 or 3 years before the usual age, sometimes at 9 or 10. Intelligence doesn't evolve in the same way.*

The adolescent who has grown too quickly endures ridicule about his proportions, he curbs signs of sexuality, is ashamed of his erections, of his wet dreams, he remains passive and timid, he stoops to match the height of his friends.

He becomes quarrelsome, quick-tempered. His need for adventure sometimes leads him to dire acts, such as running away.

IN CASES OF DELAYED PUBERTY, *there are a lot of anxieties. During recreation, or in the dormitories at boarding school, children ages 15-16 whose puberty comes late compare their size, musculature and sex organs with those of their peers and feel humiliated. Their grades may suffer from it. We repeatedly tell these young people that nothing has been lost. Today's modalities of treatment are effective.*

WHY ARE TEENAGERS DISSATISFIED WITH THEIR BODIES? *One's transformation is accompanied by a distortion of the features, pimples, first appearance of peach fuzz; but this is just a rough sketch, very far away from the final design. Teenagers are impatient and unhappy, one thinks that his hairline is no good, another that his ears stick out too much, yet another that his thighs are too fat.*

In the mirror, they make grimaces, brush their hair, imitate famous actors. Their habits betray a perpetual dissatisfaction. This is only aggravated by a persistent need to please the opposite sex.

The most convincing rite of initiation for establishing the teenager as a man is, doubtlessly, winning the heart of a young girl. Aside from satisfying his need to please, this prize puts him in the same ranking as his pals and fulfils his will to power.

WHAT DO YOU NEED TO DO TO BE LIKED, ADMIRED? *To maintain good relations with others, one must first be in tune with one's own body. You can't like others if you don't like yourself.*

DOES MASTURBATION HAVE ANY DETERMINENTAL CONSEQUENCES? *It is a normal stage in the sexuality of the adolescent. Between 12 and 16, nearly 90% of young people resort to it as an expression of their sex instinct.*

During that period of life, this instinct, which peaks at the age of 15, is quite demanding.

Our society imposes strict taboos on the adolescent. He has no other choice but to make use of his own body. He masturbates to put an end to sexual tension that can result in testicular pain.

During pleasure for one, adolescents' imagination is bursting with activity. They manufacture a dream world, starting with their daily encounters or strong impressions from their reading or from films.

With girls, masturbation is reduced to imaginative daydreaming that materializes before sleep. Although, more or less early on, a lot of them discover clitoral stimulation.

IS MASTURBATION DANGEROUS PSYCHOLOGICALLY? *No, as long as it's only a stage of sexual development. In that case, it's even useful, since boys and girls discover in it their attraction for the opposite sex. This imaginary attraction is an excellent prelude to subsequent relations.*

DOES MASTURBATION STOP BY ITSELF? *It should disappear by itself around the age of 16 or 17.*

However, some older adolescents, and even some adult males, continue to resort to it.

It is normal for an adolescent to turn to masturbation to soothe sexual tension. But such a practice can also help him survive a difficult time: if he isn't loved enough by his family, if he's in boarding school, an orphanage, or to offset the anxiety over a bad grade on an end-of-term test or some other kind of setback.

The danger in this, since there is a danger, is his getting the habit of taking refuge in himself for every sorrow or obstacle. He'll become bashful, will no longer dare to be around girls. He'll flee reality, which is never good.

Therefore, when masturbation persists beyond the age of 17, it is an expression of difficulties. The opposite sex is frightening, boys dread confronting these strange beings of a different sex: everything seems to keep them apart. They prefer to turn inward.

They should ask for help from friends, parents, a doctor. They'll have to get used to mixing with the opposite sex, which is the only sure way of not jeopardizing their sex life later.[29]

DOES MASTURBATION INCREASE OR REDUCE THE SIZE OF THE PENIS? *We can't answer yes to either of these two questions. The most recent experiments by American scientists have proven that the size of the penis has no relationship to the size or physical strength of a boy.*

In its dormant state, appreciable enough differences can be noted from one individual to another. But when the penis is erect, they become less pronounced—the size of the penis is therefore approximately the same in all individuals.[30]

---

29. Volume 17–18 years will clearly go to the limit in the expression of these cautions: masturbation leads to narcissism, which leads to homosexuality, a psychological disease and social deviance. Such is the theory and "thought" of our doctors.

30. Masters and Johnson (the only famous "American scientists" to which the Hachette text is able to allude about this subject) have, on the contrary, discovered the opposite.

The authors of the Encyclopedia wish in this case to discourage unhealthy curiosity, dangerous admiration, emasculated humiliation that would cause, apparently, fearfulness in the presence of girls. In addition, the latter must be taught that all "penises" are the same and therefore be dissuaded from playing the bird-catcher.

But to get back to the American researchers, they observed the following point (leaving us dumbfounded in the face of such "experiments"—soon state-of-the-art sexology will know as much about this as the crude sexology of women who like to fuck and homosexuals): the longer a cock is when it's limp, the less it changes size when it gets hard—all its proportions remaining the same. Example: limp cocks of around 9 cm will become hard cocks of around 14-15 cm; limp cocks measuring from 12 to 15 cm will become hard cocks of 16.5 to 18 cm.

We can see that the difference in length between limp cocks doesn't go away when they harden: they are transmitted to the differences between hard cocks, lightly decreasing or not at all.

Consequently, the dimensions are and remain quite variable, regardless of the mood of the sex object. What is the range of these differences in dimension? Up to twice the size, and even more. 99% of the hard cocks measure between 10 and 22.5 cm, depending on the individual (adults). The remaining 1% corresponds to micro- or macro-exceptions.

The extremes, of course, are in the minority. If you go hunting for them, and start considering 90% of the hard cocks rather than 99%, the range becomes narrower: 11.5 to 19.5 cm. Outside the "quagmire" of the 13-16 cm (a variation that is already enough to create a lot of discrimination, humiliation and pride), one notices two important and equal groups: firstly, the 11.5-12.5 cm, and secondly, the 17-18 cm.

(As a parenthesis, jerking off, according to Science, definitely does not wear it out and doesn't make it grow, either; maybe it ends up making cocks puff up a little fuller than they did).

It goes without saying that all these differences have no importance—but they have the misfortune of concerning a market element that is as secretive as it is overvalued. The incredible anxieties that often result from this provide the daily bread of sexologists-counselors; I hardly dare say, their fortune.

It's amusing to note that the very serious and excellent *Human Sex Anatomy* by R. L. Dickinson reported a story about a 34-cm cock: it was attached to a boy of 15.

Thus, the apprehensions about the influence of masturbation on the size of the penis are not based on any precise scientific data.

WHY IS IT SO DIFFICULT TO GET ALONG WITH MY FAMILY? *The teenager asserts his personality by opposition and identification. Opposition: to show his independence, he routinely says the opposite of what his parents say. He refuses to be guided in the choice of his friends, his reading material, his entertainment or his political opinions. He turns down Sunday outings with his dad and mom, he demands the right to go out at night.*

He wants to live his own life and do without the experience of others.

ARE PARENTS ALWAYS UNDERSTANDING? *Some parents don't react well to such an atmosphere. They don't understand these attitudes of defiance, this arrogance and impatience.*

But they should know that this antagonism doesn't put into doubt their older child's love for them—it is a demand for freedom. Despite their fear and sadness, the parents should witness this marvelous transformation of their child with love and be careful not to interfere too much. They'll encourage him to accept his responsibilities; they'll let him invite his friends to the house; they'll be careful not to come down on his enthusiasm, his taste for adventure.

But for his part, the teenager needs to make an effort to better understand his parents. Their sometimes insensitive lectures are only the proof of too much love. He'll forgive them a lot, because their love for him is strong!

The teenager should take care not to disown or reject his parents in any way. He might feel bad about it later, have regrets that might delay his adult maturity—the goal of his ambition and his struggle.

TO BECOME A MAN, IS IT NECESSARY TO REBEL AGAINST YOUR HOME ENVIRONMENT? *No, you can also emulate some models you prefer. YOUR GANG, in which the teenagers ... try to model themselves after the leader of the gang, who better embodies all their aspirations.*

A BEST FRIEND, with whom you share everything, your thoughts, desires, emotions, doubts. You imitate his habits, his mannerisms. You envy his ease with the opposite sex, his scholastic successes, his sports achievements. And you acquire some of his virtues. Then there are other models for teenagers, so much more prestigious that they seem out of reach: singers and film stars, sports idols, soap opera heroines—and, as is still the case with a lot of young people, heroes of the great novels.

Violence isn't the only way for a teenager to recover from the unrest of his situation. Games, singing, dance remain the last bastions where freedom can spread its wings.

WHEN DO YOU BECOME AN ADULT? *When you achieve independence on a number of levels.* INTELLECTUAL INDEPENDENCE: *the adolescent who is becoming a man thinks for himself, develops his personal philosophy.* INDEPENDENCE FROM THE HOME ENVIRONMENT: *this is the most difficult and most painful stage. The risk is that such independence might lead to a misunderstanding and retrigger that much-talked-about conflict between the generations.* INDEPENDENCE IN THE CHOICE OF FRIENDS AND LONG-TERM COMPANION. INDEPENDENCE, lastly, IN TERMS OF OCCUPATION *or profession: when you become capable of earning your living, you can take on the responsibilities of your private life and your role in society.*

WHAT DO PARENTS FEAR? *The path leading to independence and freedom has its snares: the parents find themselves confronted with a dilemma, when to use their authority to save their children from those dangers that they foresee, and when to let them experiment. For example, let's take the problem of pornography...*

SHOULD BOOKS WITH EROTIC ILLUSTRATIONS OR PORNOGRAPHY THAT GET PASSED AROUND ON THE SLY BE BANNED? *On principle, we are against all censorship, censorship of films, books or the press. But material that children are given often shows sexual perversions:*

these distort the beauty and bliss of the sexual act. However, such a rea-
son doesn't seem enough to justify prohibiting it. Because the teenagers
who look at these erotic nudes do so for three essential reasons; they're
trying either to satisfy their curiosity about sexual matters, to fathom the
secrets of adults or to stimulate their imagination during masturbation.
The parents should satisfy curiosity about the facts of sex. There are
hardly any secrets in this area that they shouldn't be willing to discuss.

WHY DON'T OUR PARENTS LET US CHOOSE OUR OWN PEO-
PLE TO ASSOCIATE WITH? *They're afraid that their children will be*
talked into doing bad things, or will learn bad habits from a friend
who comes from a different background—or is less balanced when it
comes to character or intelligence. Most of the time, these parents are
wrong. However, there are cases in which they're justified in fearing
the influence of a group or a friend they see as pernicious—someone
who could draw their child into some dire actions such as theft or
drug use.

The same problems pop up when it comes to going out at night.
Only a frank discussion between parents and children will resolve
these touchy problems, taking into account school schedules and good
health in general.

AT WHAT POINT IS A SIMPLE FRIENDSHIP BETWEEN A BOY
AND A GIRL NO LONGER POSSIBLE? *The desire to fool around coin-*
cides with the dawning of puberty. This is when the boys feel a strong
attraction for girls; and, similarly to Narcissus, the girls like to gaze at
themselves in the eyes of their male admirers.

This sexual awakening is happening earlier and earlier. It is
encouraged by certain kinds of liberation in our society, and the fact of
our being inundated by all sorts of erotic material: advertising, litera-
ture, the weeklies compete to be the most daring, more and more
frequently showing risqué images of nudes.

Today, at 14, one girl in nine has a brief romance and dates; twenty-five years ago, the proportion was one in a thousand.

DO GIRLS AND BOYS WANT TO FOOL AROUND FOR THE SAME REASON? *No. Fooling around (kissing and sometimes giving each other a few caresses) doesn't have the same meaning for girls: It's important for teenagers to be well aware of this.*

FOR BOYS: *the sex instinct reaches its peak between ages 16 and 20. Normal boys have demanding, pressing sexual desires, which obsess them as long as they remain unsatisfied. But two essential obstacles work against their having sexual relations with girls: on the one hand there is the continuation of schoolwork, which delays their entrance into the world—so that these young men aren't in a position to provide for a family; and on the other hand, they lack maturity. Without a good understanding of their partner, failure is usually the result. Only gradually does the fear of the other sex recede. For these two reasons, the adolescent prefers resorting to masturbation.*

CAN A BOY HAVE HIS FIRST EXPERIENCE WITH A PROSTITUTE? *Certainly, in this case, relations involve another person. But the experience isn't recommended. It's a false relationship from the beginning because the satisfaction of sexual desire is exchanged for money.*

In our society, to prove he is a man, an adolescent has no other possibility than winning the heart of a woman.

(Back to fooling around) *Fooling around is only a compromise for a boy, he has to settle for kisses and petting, whereas his need to dominate, his male aggressiveness demands total victory.*

But fooling around teaches him to calm his apprehensions, to better control his senses, and to always combine a feeling of affection and honesty with his desire.

FOR GIRLS 14–16, *sensuality is neither as demanding nor as intense. It is romantic love that is important for her. Physical pleasure comes after. Above all, she expects tender words, signs of attention that reassure her about her femininity and her capacity to please. They will carry her off into a dream world, and she will convey her feelings in confidences to a friend or in her diary.*

She doesn't feel a need to have sexual relations.

The first kiss is only a concession. Girls kiss in order to do what everybody else is doing.

Pleasure only comes next. The role of motherhood makes her very conscious of her responsibilities, and protects her from herself.

DOES FOOLING AROUND HAVE ITS DISADVANTAGES? *For the boy, it represents an improvement over masturbation. It has great value as a way of acting against homosexual tendencies.*

But a young man must understand and accept the fact that a young girl doesn't want to go beyond certain limits.

Young girls won't have to give in to curiosity, to a need to please. Fooling around reduced to the search for physical pleasure ought to be banned.

AT WHAT AGE SHOULD YOU GO TO BED WITH A GIRL? DON'T SEXUAL RELATIONS AT THIS STAGE HAVE ONLY DISADVANTAGES?

They can offer some advantages: at times they put an end to obsessions that could get in the way of your studies; they allow you to get experience, which will be indispensable at the time of marriage; finally, they allow you to move beyond homosexual tendencies, which are present in every adolescent.

But there are numerous problems. (Who to sleep with:) PROSTITUTES? *They risk turning off teenagers permanently from love.* GIRLS THEIR AGE? *Their sexual needs aren't as pressing. Besides, society is still fiercely against it.* OLDER WOMEN? An army of female initiators! There don't seem to be any counterarguments against that.

WHY SHOULD I REMAIN CELIBATE? *In our society, taboos forbidding sexual relations for adolescents persist, despite the wave of sexuality sweeping over every front. Against those taboos, the adolescent brings the force of his sex instinct, which will never be more powerful than it is at that moment.*

Sexual relations certainly are a factor in development. In relation to masturbation, they represent indisputable progress.

But it seems to us that sexual freedom can only be conceived under two conditions:

—not being penalized by a feeling of guilt or fear: each ought to take care not to underestimate the weight of education and the rules imposed by one's environment;

—assuming one's responsibilities in two frameworks: finding out about methods of contraception to eliminate the risk of pregnancy, and, if you are a boy, not wronging your partner, who doesn't always have the same reason as you to give in.

A man and a woman ought to feel mature enough to accept the consequences of their acts: the possibility of a pregnancy, the possible repercussions of these relations on going to school, the possible consequences on a psychological level. Girls don't have the same reason as men to give in (third mention).

SHOULD YOU REMAIN A VIRGIN? *Losing your virginity to satisfy simple curiosity, to imitate Dad or Mom, to do a friend a favor, or to do something that shows your independence from the home environment does not represent progress for an adolescent on the path of freedom and autonomy. In fact, the disappointments won't be far behind. A girl ends up hating herself, she realizes that she was only a sex object for her partner. Unthinkingly cynical, teenagers will reject her unceremoniously after having gotten what they wanted. In the end, freedom at the exorbitant price of low self-esteem and contempt for others—which can be accompanied by remorse towards one's parents and the fear of pregnancy—is a lot more enslaving that the constraints of families.*

WHY DO GIRLS OF 14 GO TO BED WITH BOYS? *Most often, it's not because they're looking for pleasure. They are lonely and lack or think they lack affection. These little girls who go to bed with boys are very unhappy and don't know what it means to give of yourself. They beg for affection in exhange for their body.*

IS HOMOSEXUALITY NORMAL? *A very important question. Adolescence is a turning point at which sexual tendencies are established for good. When the sex instinct explodes, a teenager has several possibilities: masturbation (a frequent tool of adolescence); fooling around (which means putting a damper on sexual impulses); actual sexual relations (difficult, seeing that the teenager lacks maturity and a sense of responsibility, and at that age it isn't always easy to find a worthwhile partner).*

It's also often more convenient to forge a friendship with a buddy of the same sex. This phase is normal and even desirable. But it is only a passing phase. There are, however, boys and girls who, for diverse reasons, don't go beyond this stage of homosexual relationships.

They are afraid of the opposite sex and don't dare approach them.

Or special circumstances, such as boarding school, have kept them away from girls.

Or their parents weren't viable models with whom to identify. The boy hasn't learned to behave like a man, nor has the girl learned to behave like a woman.

And yet everything is there. It's so much easier to achieve happiness if your behavior is in line with your sex.

One homosexual experience isn't enough to endanger your future. But the teenage years are full of snares. Certain adults (whose sex instincts went off course earlier in life) are well aware of this. They pounce upon those young people who are still trying to find their sexuality.

You should refuse to have a conversation with them, refuse to follow them, even if they seem very polite and very cultured. It's important to pass the stage of homosexual relationships quickly and to mix with the opposite sex.

EXHIBITIONISTS *expose their sex organs to young people to prove their virility to themselves. Certain* SADISTS *try to lure them away in order to satisfy their need to do harm.*

Don't go with those you don't know. Keep walking and stay calm. If the stranger insists, don't hesitate to ask for help from friends, passers-by, or an officer.

There are other sexually sick people whom you can run into on paths, in the woods or in public places like movie theaters.

The book intended for ages 14–16 ends with these "sexually sick people" whom you "can run into" (is that giving permission?).

I'm a little ashamed of having pulled together in so indigestible a hunk a group of quotations that I hadn't even intended to comment upon, because my entire book is its commentary. I devoted a lot of pages to analyzing the volume for ages 10–13; I tried to detect the ideological discourse hiding behind its friendly surface. But this time I have nothing more to do; what I took so much trouble shedding light on has in this case been said straight out by the authors. Their unbelievable patching together of grandma's louis-philippe-style morality goes beyond all the obscenities that I could say to unveil their intentions. *Complete sex information* will have had the following virtue: once again we're able to put into the hands of boys and girls a dogma that originally made even newborns snicker—and that now, nicely laced with *vaginismus, sports idols, suggestive nudes* and *gentle and timid heroines*, relaunches its attack, more spirited than ever.

No illusions, please: the authors aren't counting on their slimy arguments and homespun advice about economy to hold back adolescents who *don't know what it means to give of yourself.* The jaws of the dogma yawn widely at hell—a hell that isn't evil's, but the Order's. Absolute power for parents, vicious social taboos, impossibility of minors communicating with one another, prohibition of being at one with yourself, constraint, isolation; actions constantly curtailed, lost, liquidated in any kind of glandular-excess toilet at all; traps for autonomy in a society in which the minor, nonproducer and nonowner can't exist.

In dividing boys and girls so obsessively—men-strong-aggressive-intelligent, women-weak-submissive-stupid—the *Encyclopedia* isn't hoping that they'll copy Man and Woman for a society of inequality in which no one wants to live any more; they're merely trying to misappropriate their desires, to arm each of them in his or her fashion so that they'll go to war. War between these young males whose *aggressiveness demands total victory*, and these young females who write in their *diaries* and whose fear of parents, fear of pregnancy, fear of pain, fear of being abandoned as soon as "conquered" ruthlessly keeps them "virgins." The aggressor and the aggressed: let each live this role passionately and believe even more in the role played by the other than in his own. Desire equals fear.

Body cut in two. Human cut in two: adults/non-adults; and in two again: possessor/possessed. Then an infinity of other discriminations, one after another, erecting each law of the market; the body is no longer even what transgresses these laws, it is what keeps them alive. It invests in them in order to exist—they thrive, and they destroy it. They want the living-dead, meat on which to live as a parasite, not corpses.

What does the sex education that "defines" the "confusion" of adolescence teach? Respect for *schoolwork, good health in general,* fear of *bad associations,* boys from a *different background,* compassion and contempt for those who lost their virginity early, respect for the Family, respect for Virginity, respect for Medicine, respect for the social order, respect for the thrilling stages that will take the adolescent from the state of being an ugly and ridiculous model of frustration to being an irreproachable and handsome Father. Your bodies are a rough sketch, your face is a clumsy imitation, your brain is made of smoke, your desires are bestial and would corrupt you. This shower of spit in the face of kids, these pages and pages one upon the other with nothing but words of hate, lying, contempt; it's all too much to "forgive" those who "love" so much.

All we need do, one more time, is to compare this lovely discourse of "understanding" from which I've copied the essential with these four little words: sexual majority at 14. The French torrent of repression, and Danish liberalization. Every sentence of the good French counselors answers *no* to what, elsewhere, has finally become *yes*.

But I don't want to dwell on this comparison. Enviable as it may seem to us, Danish reform is certainly not a revolution; it will relieve a lot of suffering, but it won't change the source of it, at least not in the short term. It changes nothing, in fact, about the reproduction of the order. The child, the preadolescent will remain family-centric, put on the sidelines and oedipalized; a individual of 14 who will have the right to have sex will only have that sex after 14 years of training in *commerce*.

Of course, as I've indicated, over there the family is more open. But this balancing of parental power is probably the case only after the first years of the child's life. Because the murders of the very small, with the large amount of abuse that they imply, are currently as numerous in Denmark as elsewhere. Thus the "baby" plays the same role as it does in the libidinal system of

French parents, for example. And this symptom of parental defects is even more significant when it's observed in a country whose democratic structures, freedoms, tolerances, are at the forefront of Western capitalism and the passage to happiness for everyone—the spirit of "let's all be owners" and "we only exploit what's outside."

These oedipal murders prove to us that an easing up of institutions changes nothing about the order and its defects; soft or hard, it produces the same effects. The familial order—corporeal capitalism—can only be reproduced through suffering, frustration and death. The suicides don't diminish either: commercial pleasures, even if they are infinitely more numerous than ours, don't restore life. And a sexuality, a desire, a corporality that is formed and indoctrinated for entrance into the laws of the market, production and ownership, remain just as alienated, as misappropriated whether the laws of this market are supple or implacable.

An easing up of the order signifies an "altruistic" and "objective" effort to remedy certain of its vices, instead of denying them as we in our country do; but it comes down to keeping that order in place.

Note that the order in question no longer needs to weigh as heavily on all human behavior and that some of the things that overwhelm the body can be relieved—because the order is maintained only by its essential pillars. It's like moving from a colossal architecture in the old style, where the structure rests on powerful foundations supported by enormous buttresses, to a "modern" structure, adroitly designed in such a way that its mass rests on a base that is slender, subtle in appearance, eccentrically minuscule in relation to the structure but supporting that structure more rigorously, more solidly than any massive plinth has ever been able to do.

To the extent that society becomes conscious of the only

points of support on the bodies of the exploited that are indispensable, it allows itself, here and there, the humanism to remove constraints that have become superfluous. These reforms are like rewards that a "good" exploiting state grants, a justice that it recognizes, a legitimization that it offers itself. The order is likeable, it does no more than it needs to maintain itself and thrive.

And all the conservative countries are drooling with envy at the small nations that have already constructed the Modern and Functional Order. We'll have it, too, someday, we hope; it's the future itself of the society of exploitation, its survival depends upon it. And to the extent that the dominant class, which by principle is resistant to all innovation, senses an urgency to reform one or another of its foundations, we're bound to see the voting in of small freedoms that will make us melt with gratitude. How good the Masters have become!

In the long run, however, I think that Danish reform might constitute a completely new element of civilization, capable of calling into question the old sexual capitalism. The first generation to benefit from that freedom will content themselves with exercising it more or less strictly according to the laws of the market they were trained to accept. But perhaps later, the sexual market itself will be transformed by this, meaning that it will gradually be dismantled.

The new families of the men and women who will have obtained sexual freedom starting at age 14 won't resemble ours. The child is bound to have a different role, a much better status. The libidinal misappropriations of the child by the family will no longer have the ferocity, the brutal determination that they have in the homes of the frustrated and guilt-ridden, who respect an order that was cudgeled into them.

This is an optimistic hypothesis, because if adolescents see their desire standing in the way of a market as tough as the one that adults are subjected to everywhere; if they're not capable of inventing their own deprivatizing anticommercial freedoms that are the freedom of desire itself; they will only know pain, humiliation, frustration, and they will wait for the age of marriage-ownership with the same impatience they had about wanting to have sex.

A long time will be needed to determine whether this reform is in the end only a new bandage on an unchanged wound, or whether it has the capacity to heal gradually. In other words, if it is a process of reproduction of the order, or if it has the power to begin its true and complete transformation.

In any case, the hope that lies at the end of sexual freedom for minors is that their children will no longer have to be liberated: they'll be born that way and will remain so. They alone will know how to remake a society they have inherited without having to endure its chains. No reform, if it can alleviate these chains, our chains, today, has any real meaning or stature unless it can keep us from passing them on to anyone else tomorrow.

In addition, the sexual freedom of the minor is, in my opinion, the first of the political problems to pose: with it, and only with it, can the process of the reproduction of power be checked and cancelled. When it comes to the sexuality of minors, all the countries of exploitation, whether capitalist or communist, socialist or fascist, have the same ideology, which involves the familial sacrifice of the child for the satisfaction of those who are already exploited. And everywhere the body has the same status, suffers the same proscriptions, the same insipid or police-like indoctrination, whether it's the unctuous style of the West or the military style of the Chinese; and from this comes the essential importance of any struggle that, releasing childhood and adolescence from the clutch of adult power, disinvesting desire of any quest for ownership, commandeering and profit, can undermine the domination of exploitive structures—because obedience, privatization, attainment of power will no longer be the only chances imposed upon the existence of desire.

OVEREXPOSED
Sylvère Lotringer

With a new introduction by the author and an additional chapter.

The most perverse perversions are not always those one would expect. Originally conceived as an American update to Foucault's *History of Sexuality*, *Overexposed* is even more outrageous and thought-provoking today than it was twenty years ago when it was first published. Half-way between *Dr. Strangelove* and *Clockwork Orange*, this insider's exposition of cutting-edge cognitive behavioral methods is a hallucinating document on the limits presently assigned to humanity. It also offers a reflection on the overall 'obscenity' of contemporary society where everything, and not just sex, is exposed in broad daylight to quickly sink into complete indifference.

"*Overexposed* is an engrossing description of sexual conditioning condoned by the state. A fascinating book."
— William Burroughs

6 x 9 • 192 pages • ISBN-13: 978-1-58435-045-3 • $14.95

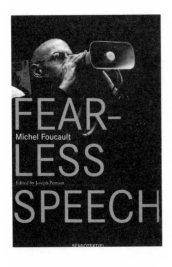

FEARLESS SPEECH
Michel Foucault, Edited by Joseph Pearson

Still unpublished in France, *Fearless Speech* concludes the genealogy of truth that Foucault pursued throughout his life, starting with his investigations in *Madness and Civilization*, into the question of power and its technology. The expression "fearless speech" is a rough translation of the Greek parrhesia, which designates those who take a risk to tell the truth; the citizen who has the moral qualities required to speak the truth, even if it differs from what the majority of people believe and faces danger for speaking it.

Parrhesia is a verbal activity in which a speaker expresses his personal relationship to truth through frankness instead of persuasion, truth instead of flattery, and moral duty instead of self-interest and moral apathy.

4 1/2 x 7 • 128 pages • ISBN-13: 978-1-58435-011-8 • $11.95

POLYSEXUALITY
Edited by François Peraldi

Originally conceived as a special *Semiotext(e)* issue on homosexuality at the end of the 70s, "Polysexuality" quickly evolved into a more complex and iconoclastic project whose intent was to do away with recognized genders altogether, considered far too limitative. It started by blowing wide open all sexual classifications, inventing unheard-of categories, regrouping singular features into often original configurations, like Corporate Sex, Alimentary Sex, Soft or Violent Sex, and Discursive Sex. Mixing documents, interviews, fiction, theory, poetry, psychiatry and anthropology, "Polysexuality" became the encyclopedia sexualis of a continent that is still emerging.

Includes work by Alain Robbe-Grillet, Félix Guattari, Paul Verlaine, William S. Burroughs, Georges Bataille, Pierre Klossowski, Roland Barthes, Tony Duvert and more.

7 x 10 • 300 pages • ISBN-13: 978-1-570-27011-6 • $14.95

DAVID WOJNAROWICZ

☐ A definitive history of five or six years on the lower east side

Interviews by Sylvère Lotringer, Edited By Giancarlo Ambrosino

DAVID WOJNAROWICZ
A Definitive History of Five or Six Years on the Lower East Side
Edited by Giancarlo Ambrosino

In February 1991, the artist David Wojnarowicz (1954–1992) and the philosopher Sylvère Lotringer met in a borrowed East Village apartment to conduct a long-awaited dialogue on Wojnarowicz's work. Already suffering the last stages of AIDS, David saw his dialogue with Lotringer as a chance to set the record straight on his art and life. Lotringer then spent the next several years gathering additional commentary on Wojnarowicz's life and work from those who knew him best—the friends with whom he collaborated.

Included are the personal testimony from Mike Bildo, Steve Brown, Richard Kern, Carlo McCormick, Ben Neill, Kiki Smith, Nan Goldin, Marguerite van Cook, and others. What emerges from these interviews is a surprising insight into something art history knows, but systematically hides: the collaborative nature of the work of any "great artist."

7 x 10 • 220 pages • Color • ISBN-13: 978-1-58435-035-4 • $29.95